Free-Progress-Education

*A futuristic vision of
self-directed, project-oriented,
direct-democratic, and non-hierarchical,
learning communities
from primary education to academic research*

Marco Masi Ph.D.[*]

Table of Contents

Introduction to the ideal of a Free-Progress-Education

Rethinking education as a precondition for the progress of mankind

The survival of a humanity which is not willing to change is far from guaranteed. In a globalized and interconnected world, we won't be allowed to continue with the same mindset, habits, institutions and policies that we have maintained for the last couple of centuries. Economic or social reforms will not be enough. Sophisticated scientific-technological machinery such as artificial intelligence (AI) or humans on Mars won't save us, either. The ever-increasing complexity of our social, economic and material infrastructures will become out of control despite – and, eventually, because of – an equally increasingly complex rationalized and digitalized organization. Humanity must choose: Go beyond and accept not merely a superficial external change, but also a mental, psychological and spiritual transmutation, or become part of an enslaving machine which sooner rather than later will lead to a catastrophic relapse, if not to self-annihilating scenarios.

These challenges range from a global financial system that is rapidly collapsing under its own weight to an ecosystem that might be destroyed by a mindless species which is trampling everything it finds in its path, from terrorism, to national or ethnic conflicts that are spreading throughout the world, to the more subtle but no less insidious problems of the psychological dimension that are plaguing the human race.

If humanity will not become a more peaceful species, weapons of mass destruction might wipe it out or send it back to the stone ages. Peace treaties, new political world orders or high-ranking presidential summits might temporarily postpone conflicts but cannot, in the long run, avoid war and potential self-destructive behaviors. Science and technology will play a decisive role in converting environmentally destructive production means and polluting energy sources into clean and sustainable economic infrastructures. However, it is an illusion to believe this alone will be enough. If the next couple of generations do not develop a renewed inner contact and love for Nature as part of their own being and spiritual essence, all the sciences, green policies and economies or international climate summits may result in the helpless inability to avoid disastrous climate change and a lethal global poisoning of earth, water and air.

The same applies to supposedly new forms and conceptions of economic orders. The right-wing ideal of a (more or less capitalist) self-regulatory competition-based economy, which supposedly distributes wealth according to meritocratic principles, as well as the left-wing ideal of finding socio-political machinery able to redistribute wealth according to principles of equality, have always led, at best, to only very partial successes. An economic barbarism of commercial exploitation in an overpopulated world remains an ever-present reality and the divide between rich and poor has only grown and seems unstoppable.

To resolve these global issues, new thinking and feeling are necessary. Skills like creativity, imagination, genius, originality, inspiration and contemplation, as well as a completely new vision of the future and how we are supposed to get there, are urgently needed. However, our present institutional educational and academic system systematically sets aside these skills or even represses them.

Humankind must change its mind and soul from the inside-out by stopping to look for a miraculous technocratic formula which believes an outer perfection could lead to its harmony and happiness. This change won't be possible if the coming generations are educated by the same principles, mindset and institutional order which frame the present educational system and which, in turn, frame their minds. One of the necessary actions to save human civilization is to embrace the key function of education. If we do not soon allow for new forms of education which contemplate the individual human being in its spiritual dimension and which do not focus solely on the intellectual development of the child and teenager, then (regardless of how rationally, scientifically and technologically well-educated they might therefore become), humankind will continue to remain cognitively utterly unable to avoid preventable catastrophic setbacks due to war, environmental collapse and economic or psychological meltdowns.

The recent worldwide "School Strike for Climate" movement (also known as "Fridays for Future") in which school students decided to not attend classes and instead to take part in demonstrations which demand action to prevent further global warming and climate change, is quite a symptomatic event. Young people (more or less unconsciously) regard school as a place that no longer prepares them for the future and the real world in which they will soon live. Despite its not being explicitly rationalized and verbalized, it is clear that they feel their education is not appropriate for dealing with the pressing issues our modern society must urgently deal with.

In this context, education is central because if the chains which actually are enslaving it won't be cut, all the other existential issues that humanity must urgently and sustainably govern will find, in the best-case scenario, only very superficial and temporary solutions, or will result in self-destruction in the worst case. Without a completely new education paradigm, the global problems we are facing can't be settled. A new educational paradigm allowing new generations to become more flexible in their thinking and actions is a precondition of the resolution of global threats. If the Gordian knot of education doesn't undergo a deep and systemic structural change which eliminates imposed curricula, grades and preordered learning paths onto all, without opening itself to the curiosity and inner potential of the child and the individual genius which hides in every one of us, humanity might still reach high material and technological achievements, but will finally become, itself, a machine – a 'borg-society' which ultimately will end like the dinosaurs.

The good news, however, is that if we embrace such change, we, as a species, will not only allow ourselves to survive but will be able to go much further than what our wildest imagination can think of. It is not about fixing and oiling the same machine, and not even about inventing a new one, but about laying the foundations for a new luminous and harmonious future on Earth which can manifest itself if our inner and spiritual powers can finally be unleashed.

Motivation for the ideal of a Free-Progress-Education

"You cannot teach a man anything, you can only help him find it within himself."
Galileo Galilei (1564–1642)

Galileo had this insight about four centuries ago. Our schools and universities are, however, still modelled on an obsolete framework of values, a framework that had as its sole purpose the creation of an obedient and malleable citizenry fitted for commercial productivity and military efficiency. While we have seen, in our own times, dictatorships fall and new freedoms blossom, and, thanks to the Internet, increasingly liberated individual self-expression, schools and higher education still remain governed by an unchanged authoritarian mindset that considers the creative potential of the individual at best a secondary aspect, and in most cases fears it as a threat. Learning continues to be mainly based on a dry, mechanical process that ignores the creative and spiritual dimensions of the human being.

In my personal experience as schoolteacher and tutor for first-year college students, I could observe how deep the lack of critical thinking is in too many young students, and how an entire generation has lost their creative potential. Most young people today are 'learning consumers', not thinking creators or producers. Many got a degree with the best grades, and yet have lost almost all their ability to think out of the box. They accept blindly the mainstream theories, or repeat blindly that of the so called 'free thinking' 'independent' media of the opposite side, wait for orders from the top, and are only able to solve problems (sometimes quite efficiently, indeed), but don't feel any desire to ask questions. Several act like obedient and subservient soldiers who feel gratified at how quick and efficient they are in executing the given tasks. But they no longer have visions or any mental ability to look beyond their narrow borders towards new horizons.

Many are proud to be part of some prestigious university or to be employed in a powerful corporation, but have lost their soul and a healthy, sceptical attitude towards the system they have willingly agreed to be slaves of. But I'm not blaming them. In the prison camps for children, called 'schools', most youngsters are subjected against their will, by the system they were born into, to a subtle but permanent and incessant social conditioning that forces them to kill their own creative self-development, self-expression, and potential for creative self-organization. In order to survive, these children have to conform to that system by sacrificing their ability to think critically and to be creative, to such a degree that they are no longer aware of this loss. If asked what they really want, even at an advanced age, the typical answer is *'I don't know'*. We are looking at an entire generation of young people 'zombified' by a programme that repressed since childhood any self-unfoldment, a generation that, if allowed to become suddenly free, would stand there with a big question mark over it, and falling either in total passivity without knowing what to do, or into lawless chaos.

And yet, I know that the contrary is true also. The new generations, and even more the coming ones, are different than those only twenty or thirty years ago. The new children will increasingly refuse to participate in a standardized activity which supposedly fits for all. More and more teen agers are questioning the system their parents accepted almost without criticism. Fewer and fewer youngsters will follow blindly the educational path the state or some private school system has planned for them already before their birth. Many children will live much more inwards and may manifest their dissatisfaction not in words but eventually through illnesses, mental pathologies, rebellion, truancy, etc. The future of humanity won't be characterized so much by new super technologies, as by the rise of a new spiritual and more intuitive generation of humans who will be determined to go beyond a strictly analytical, industrialized and commercial society. The coming generations will not be fulfilled only with a job and some spare time, they will do whatever they can to think and act from the soul, not just from their mind. They will feel the desire to connect beauty and arts with science and spirituality and conceive of a society where the collective and the individual have to be harmonized into a Unity in Diversity.

The present century old encrusted industrial, commercial and political establishment feels the pressure of these new generations. That is why it resists strenuously and tightens its grip by imposing even more standardization, uniformity without diversity, even less freedom of self-expression in schools and academia. It is a natural reaction of a huge matrix, a giant octopus which still has its powerful tentacles in every corner of control and power in the system. On top of that, in some countries, college students have to pay for exponentially increasing tuition fees. In the US, as of 2017, the student loan debt has become a $1.3 trillion crisis. The average of the 12.4 million student loan borrowers graduates with a loan debt between $10,000 and $25,000, and about 2 million students have a debt greater than $100,000. (1) Many students actually do not graduate at all due to their loan debt. They either drop out or simply stop going ... and they still have all their debt. How can someone study, learn and work serenely if his/her future prospect is that of drowning in college debt?

A change from this state of affairs is clearly long overdue.

But the crisis we are going to discuss here is not merely financial. When we speak out for a 'free education' ideal we are not just considering an education free of charge. Much more is at stake.

The world, on the global scale, is transforming rapidly. If mankind is to survive, and progress towards a species capable of sustainable development, the masses will have to transform, not just a handful of individuals who direct them. They will no longer be an army of obedient subjects happy to take orders from a tiny elite that has kept them in a state of thraldom, telling them what is good or bad, true or false. Such a subjugation is being perpetuated through the brainwashing implemented through the current educational system, and, to a large extent, helped by the mass media. Society at large will have to grow out of its present cocoon into a living, pulsating organism in which individuals are able to think out of the box, to act beyond solving problems, to ask fundamental questions, to discriminate between the thoughts of others and their own, and to look beyond the horizons imposed by the convention-driven, narrow-minded blackboard establishment.

Huge challenges await us, and we must soon find completely new transformative solutions. But this transformation won't happen unless education is liberated first. We urgently need a school and university system that is not an indoctrinating, repressive and exploiting institution, but a place for personal development, where students can awake to their inner intelligence, recover their mental faculties, and express their unique potential to liberate talents, individual freedom, and everyone's 'inner call'. Being free from hierarchical structures, such a system may be confidently expected to foster and nurture self-motivation and initiative, and provide a platform for free, unfettered expression of one's potential and individuality. It would also be where new forms of learning and teaching are experienced, in an environment favouring lifelong learning by doing, creative learning by teaching, and enabling everyone to learn to learn. In other words, it would be a place where there would be no compulsion to learn, where imagination replaces bookish knowledge, where everyone is free to progress by learning what he or she feels they want to learn, and where there is no academic path forced onto the students from an institution's or generation's old, bureaucratic laws.

The actual problem may well be that virtually all of the science of education which goes under the name of 'pedagogy' is almost exclusively focused on primary and secondary schools. Also the so-called democratic schools based on the model of Summerhill or Sudbury Valley School are rarely organized to deliver a high school preparation, and rarely commit any resources or attention to examining new concepts and educational methods for undergraduate and graduate students and beyond. There is no rational explanation for this state of affairs. It is a centuries-old encrusted dogma that pedagogy is only for children. It has its roots in an idea that the 'real' learning for the adult can't be done otherwise than in its present form, and in a mentality that does not question the needs of the individual, and is only interested in the uniform organization of the state, the economy, and the masses. Still equally strongly engraved is the belief that after school, once young people have enrolled at a college or university, there is to be no further reflection on possible alternative ways to learn and apprehend other than the present, given one: read, exercise, repeat the lecture, take your exam, and hope for the best grade.

While it is considered quite normal that schoolteachers should learn the theory and practice of pedagogy and didactics, the requirements in almost all universities to become a professor have nothing to do with the teaching quality that he or she will deliver in the college lecture hall. The number of articles published, the author's academic credentials, scientific achievements and awards won have sometimes some relevance, but the decisive factors affecting one's chances of being selected are their ability to find funds for the research the department could profit from, and the political power connection with other faculty members. The pedagogical and didactical capability to transfer knowledge and become an inspiration for students isn't contemplated at all as a criterion for professorship. And yet, officially, we are told that the main function of a professor in a university should be that of teaching.

It is no coincidence that, while an increasing number of children have ADHD, depression, or even burnout symptoms starting already in middle school, graduate and Ph.D. students reflect similar mental disorders when attending college or university. Children's an teens' suicides correlate with the school calendar. Research shows how psychiatric breakdowns and suicide attempts increase in the school time period. (2) According to a recent study, one third of Ph.D. students are at risk of having or developing a psychiatric disorder, especially depression. (3) (4) The work load and lack of support from tutors, stress associated with getting papers published, and the bullying behaviour or lack of useful feedback from supervisors are cited as the primary causes. Another study from 2014 highlighted how *"graduate students experience significant amounts of stress and anxiety, and their suicidal behaviour is strongly characterized by depression, hopelessness, desperation, lack of control, and eating problems."* (5) Levels of burnout among university staff are higher than in general working populations. More than 40% of postgraduate students report symptoms of depression, emotion or stress-related problems, high levels of stress and other mental health issues. (6) Unfortunately, some students are so affected that they eventually commit suicide. (7) An eloquent case was that of Francis A. Dolan, a postdoc of the Dublin Institute for Advanced Studies, in Ireland, who committed suicide in 2011. His friend, Oliver J. Rosten, dedicated the acknowledgments of a paper to his memory with the following words: *"I am firmly of the conviction that the psychological brutality of the post-doctoral system played a strong underlying role in Francis' death."* Dolan felt pressured to pursue mainstream research rather than topics a bit off the beaten path. *"It was a form of hell for him"*, Rosten says. (8) Two journals refused to include his acknowledgment but Rosten could convince a third editor to do so.

The reason these problems go almost unnoticed or remain taboo in higher education institutes, and are less felt in our society than those plaguing state schools, is that adults tend to repress their feelings, can better hide their sufferance than children, and have already learned in school to adapt rather than to complain. However, this doesn't make the facts any less real. It is time that pedagogues consider the psychological well-being among students in universities as important as that of pupils in primary schools. It is time to understand that these looming issues won't be solved by sending children or students to a therapist or simply holding panel discussions on topics like stress reduction or writing a résumé. We will argue throughout this book that the problem is, at its core, a systemic one.

Attempts to change things internally, from the inside of the conventional structures, have clearly shown that the current school and university paradigm won't allow itself to be reformed, because it is in its intrinsic essence an authoritarian system. *'Problems cannot be solved with the same mindset that created them,'* said Albert Einstein. There are too many personal and group interests ranged on the side of the status quo to permit reforms in the system. Moreover, as modern brain studies have shown, it is difficult to leave behind old mental habits, and take new paths and question the old behavioural and mental patterns. The same inertia afflicts the established educational system. I do not envisage just a simple, cosmetic reform. There have been enough such. The problem is not about the good guys or bad guys. The problem is systemic. I'm talking about a peaceful but radical 'Copernican revolution in education' that should overcome a century-old system at its roots. Only a radical transformation that grows and develops from new pedagogical ideals and structures built from scratch would have a chance to change the prevailing paradigm.

I'm quite convinced that the prevailing thinking we find dominating school and higher education, and the academic system in general, is doomed, and will sooner or later crumble under its own weight, as we have seen dictatorships, monarchies, or theocracies do.

We must envisage a new school and university as a freely self-developing self-determined learning place and community where new forms of pedagogical and didactical approaches are tested. I will focus on self-structured forms of learning and self-directed processes. Here, the professors will be replaced by 'learning mentors' who have no authority, but become 'helpers' and 'facilitators'. Students won't be forced into age-graded classrooms, but will join a group of their own free choice, establish their own curriculum, and choose freely their learning material, after having done away with a need for the sanction of a bureaucratic and hierarchical system. New pedagogical and didactical forms will be applied, such as the self-organized learning environment (SOLE), flip teaching methods, learning by teaching, un-conferences and spontaneous teamwork initiated by 'group formation camps'.

Moreover, it stands to reason that only through the abolition of exams, grades, and degrees, among several other things, will it become possible to foster creativity, intuition, and real forms of learning, and help these values flourish again in academia. In the new education paradigm, certificates would lose their perceived significance, and be replaced by learning portfolios which testify to the student's abilities and research achievements along a project-based study path. Also, some thought will be devoted to a possible future infrastructure and architectonic model that could foster effectively a dynamic interdisciplinary and trans-cultural Free-Progress-Education (FPE)[1] paradigm that will be considered and identified in a system of interconnected free-learning residential communities.

We, as a society, stand in front of several global challenges. For a peaceful future, it will be necessary to recognize education as a priority for society as a whole, and as an important resource, and to engage collectively in favour of it. Too much time has already been wasted in thinking in terms of an incremental system reform, of a step-by-step amelioration of the given structures, and of new laws and rules that should from time to time regulate and amend the present paradigm. But this only scratches the surface, and amounts to a medication which cures the symptoms but ignores the root causes of the problem. It doesn't take us much further ahead than the educational mindset of the 18th–19th century. There have been hundreds of education reforms worldwide for two centuries now without changing really the essence of it because, as Oren Harari used to say: *"The electric light did not come from the continuous improvement of candles"*. Or, as the Austrian-American management consultant Peter Drucker used to say, *"Management is doing things right; leadership is doing the right things."* Rather than giving up deeply ingrained preconceived ideas and choosing to do the right things, our managerial education system is largely devoted to trying (sometimes desperately) to do the wrong things right. Later, we find ourselves wondering why, after decades of reforms and attempts to fix issues, we are left feeling as though the "righter" one does (the wrong) things, the "wronger" those things become.

We must learn instead to think in terms of revolutionary transformations and sudden nonlinear intrinsic system changes, questioning it at its root, at its basic foundations. We should revise our thought processes, those with which we grew up and have taken for

---

[1] As to the origin of the name 'Free Progress Education' please refer to the endnote of the book.

granted since childhood, even if it was something as simple as 1+1=2. Only a systemic and paradigmatic change, accompanied by a revision of our most basic convictions, without being afraid of reconsidering everything from the ground up, down to the essence of the outdated system itself, can lead us further along the path of real, meaningful learning.

The present document is also a call to action. It invites all who are keen to contribute their skills and expertise to making this dream a reality to come forward to help in the creation of a fully fledged free-progress learning community.

A personal preamble

My learning path from elementary school to post-doc research

As a personal preamble, I might point out that my interest in the subject of education originated in my quite disappointing experiences while an undergraduate, graduate, and Ph.D. student at universities, where no place was left for a free intellectual development, and no freedom to discover and explore, and where no joy of self-learning was allowed. And it is perhaps because of my innate thirst for freedom and independence since childhood that I can't remember to have had a much better feeling at school either. Therefore, even if you might not relate it to your youth which was (hopefully) conditioned by more encouraging educational experiences, and even at the cost of appearing the 'weepy guy' who seems continuously to feel sorry for himself, let me present a brief summary of my personal experiences from childhood to adulthood.

They began in the first years of elementary school, shortly after kindergarten. I was fascinated with birds. I can't explain why, but I felt passionately that I should know all there was to know about them—their names, their species, and their lives. When I asked my teachers if I could carry out research on birds and read up on them, I was told that sure I could, but I would have to wait a couple of years still, while learning to read! '*How can you learn something about birds if you can't even read?*', was the answer. Sure, that sounds extremely rational, doesn't it? But apart from the fact that I never learned anything about birds, neither the couple of years after, nor during all the time at school, it became very clear that it was only an excuse, more precisely a lie, told to a child in order to control his innate curiosity and bring him back to obedience. Why not have learning to read by letting a child study ornithology? Would that really be an impossible solution? Bureaucratically speaking, it was indeed: the system did not allow for separate paths, everyone had to learn from the same books and in the same way. That is why I had to learn, like everyone else, from extremely boring grammar books with ridiculous dialogues like *"Hello, my name is Udo. I am Ina, what is your name? What time is it? Dora drives a car. Peter asks Dora…"*, and dozens of similar idiotic phrases, which had to be written down and repeated parrot fashion by children who, perhaps, could instead have learned all that much better and faster if their inner desire to know much more fascinating things about the world had been fulfilled. After all, children learn to speak exercising their communication skills with others and interacting with and in the world. Why is it forbidden then to learn reading by studying something which tells me about the real world, instead of going through abstract grammar books? This was one of the first impressions that left a deep trace on me, and marked the beginning of a long journey in an educational matrix, whose illusionary and delusionary aspects were, however, to reveal themselves to my consciousness much later.

In another couple of episodes that remained in my mind I recall what happened on the few occasions when I was allowed to effectively follow my interests. When I did so, the reaction spoke volumes. During a class in geography I was once allowed to investigate the birth and death of stars. In a rapture of enthusiasm I wrote a report which I read in front of the class about the evolution of stars, from the first collapse of the gas nebulae to the last stages of nuclear burning, which is characterized by that strange dance of contraction and expansion phases, eventually ending in a supernova explosion. My teacher was shocked. Since she was absolutely ignorant in astronomy, instead of informing herself on how things really work, she had nothing better to say than that I was fantasizing.

A similar experience happened when, for the first time, our maths and physics teacher dared to open a little door in favour of self-learning, allowing everyone in the class to pursue their own interest on a topic of their choice. While most seemed to be confused and felt stressed in adjusting to a new (even though only temporarily so) 'learning by doing' activity, I was thrilled, and immediately chose to begin research on electronic logic gates, i.e. the kind of circuits that are at the base of every CPU in computers. With the NAND gates I then showed how it is possible to build a 'Flip Flop', i.e. a bi-stable electronic circuit, or in other terms a single bit of memory. I was fascinated by the fact that computers have a memory, and wanted absolutely to know how it works. I was able to explain this in detail, and remember how all the class listened in a surreal silence to every word I had to say, and certainly not because of the content (I doubt they were particularly interested in knowing what AND, OR, XOR, and NAND gates are), but probably because they heard in my voice the passion for knowledge and discovery that came from my mouth, even though I wasn't really aware of it at that time. But, for some reason, all that was not digested well by my teacher, since (he said) I had '*only repeated something already known*'. That confused me, and continues to confuse me to this day, and at the time caused an uproar of protest by my classmates (a rare case of solidarity I was not used to). I certainly had not expected that kind of objection in an institution which had always fostered only a mechanical repetition of notions and had always killed off every attempt at creative thinking.

I was then about 15 years old, and the desire to learn new things was not only always there but, worse, it directed itself to more complex topics at the college or university levels. But that tendency was crushed quickly and efficiently, not through an imposition of rules, but by a triggering of the fears and apprehensions of a timid, insecure teenager. *'You are too young. You cannot understand',* was the usual argument. My family members were not particularly authoritarian, but they were not supportive either. I remember what happened when I insisted on reading a book on the theory of relativity: from my father came the same objection, and my uncle, whenever he saw me with one of Einstein's popular books in my hands, would shout as if obsessed, *'He can't understand, he can't understand!'* And indeed I could not understand where the formulas Einstein wrote in that booklet came from (Lorentz transformations), and I believed that they must be obvious and intuitive to everyone, except me. Only later did I realize that Einstein hadn't made it clear that he had just written them down omitting the proof that, by the way, can only be found in a university-level textbook.

The restraints that afflicted my generation, with its adherence to rigidly age-determined access to segments of a preassigned learning path, will (one hopes) no longer hold back coming generations. Those restraints will no longer find acceptance, and will vanish.

During pre-college school, there were dozens of other similar episodes. I never was a particularly brilliant student. Most of the time, I performed low in school or not much better than average and eventually concluded that I must be stupid and lazy. Only much later did it surface to my mind that perhaps this was because I was too fixed in trying to be 'brilliant' instead of being myself.

My real clash with the dry and encrusted education system came with my enrolment in the first years of my physics university studies. Destiny kindly (and I don't use that word lightly, mindful of how I sense real kindness in what was to follow) assigned to me the most authoritarian among my professors, who imposed their own topics that were almost useless for a real understanding of physics, and who resembled mediaeval autocrats who did what they wished without fear of legal consequences. I went through all of that boring and futile rigmarole. The worst-case scenario seemed to be specifically designed for me. For instance, my professor of calculus did not allow for questions during or after lectures. After having gone through an awful set of sterile notions thrown on the blackboard in an incomprehensible way, if a student asked for clarifications, he would answer: *'You don't understand? Study!'* I spent a whole year studying exclusively point-set topology, without learning anything about derivatives, or integral calculus—a huge waste of time that could have been better used if I had followed my intuitive feeling to deepen my knowledge of group theory, and which indeed could have been much more productive for me when studying quantum mechanics. Calculus II was not much better. I had the honor of being a student of a professor who decided that never ever would more than 10% of his students be allowed to pass his exams. You could answer all questions correctly, but if you happened to fall outside that 10% limit, you would find yourself failed under his inscrutable criteria. The course in linear algebra was all about projective geometry, quadrics, and conics, indeed nice topics, but itself almost devoid of all the other important notions a physicist badly needs. They called this 'freedom to teach', but has anyone considered the legitimate question of whether there should also be a *freedom to learn?*

What struck me more than anything else, however, was how I had to go through the full gamut of the 'shut up and calculate' philosophy. I breathed that philosophy and lived that philosophy in every cell of my body. What I am talking about is the kind of cultural and epistemological attitude in modern physics that avoids a 'framing of hypotheses' approach that Isaac Newton had deprecated (but secretly practised, as lots of historical documents clearly show). As well as steering clear of questions such as why things are as they are, that line of thinking avoids a serious philosophical search for deeper meaning. All that matters is being able to make calculations and faithfully reproduce complicated sequences of equations supposed to describe the physical world! No wonder theoretical physics today finds itself stuck in a Platonic hyper-uranium that seems unable to go beyond the standard model of particle physics. The shut-up-and- calculate paradigm, I have felt throughout my college career, is a denial of an aspect of human nature itself. If you look at the world from the point of view of a machine, you are likely to end up like a machine, and find yourself banging your head on an impenetrable wall of mysteries, like those we now face with modern quantum gravity theories, and which are showing up to be failures one after another. We are going to have to pay heavily for misjudging the seriousness of this perspective. My interest were in tensor analysis, Lie algebras, and differential geometry, and I particularly wanted to deepen my knowledge of philosophical issues such as the relativity paradoxes and the foundations of quantum mechanics. Instead, I found I was wasting a colossal amount of time on distributions (generalized functions), and neither the physics department nor the philosophy department had a course that I was interested in. Even a timid attempt to discuss the issues was dismissed as a waste of time. Worse, the concepts—mountains of them—that I was forced to learn for exam after exam turned out to be utterly useless for my intellectual development, and none of them has remained in my mind. Happily, that belongs to the past, to another era, before the arrival of research on quantum computers and quantum information, and, fortunately, we now have a changed atmosphere.

The day arrived where I could no longer bear it. I left university for several years and went to work in turns as a dispatch rider, a popular science lecturer in a city planetarium (the only job I ever enjoyed, even if underpaid), and even a paperboy, and survived in one way or another. But there was an inner call, a spiritual longing, a thirst, and a doubt present in me. I felt dissatisfied, out of place. This inner tension reached a new, almost schizophrenic breaking point, so that I returned back to university. I learned to hate academia, while, at the same time, I loved what it studied. With a distressing but constant rhythm, I took one exam after another on subjects that I felt had nothing to do with what I had in my mind, and deeper in my soul. Just imagine being forced to build a radio in our electronics course, or having to learn chemistry (does it really make sense to impose chemistry on every physicist?), whereas I wanted to build a seismograph *('Oh, that's not allowed, we are democratic here, everyone must do the same thing,'* they told me), or, in chemistry, learn something about biophysics.

And finally I made it. After about 15 years (yes, 15....), I graduated with a thesis in astrophysics. That was one of the rare occasions when I could really express myself, and enjoyed learning and studying, since I was relatively free to do my own research. In fact, a couple of articles were published from that research on the Oort comet cloud dynamics in a galactic potential. But graduation did not make me happy, quite the contrary. How was it that it took so long? How did others succeed much better than me, and many of them managed to be hired by important international institutions? I felt unworthy and depressed. And especially too 'old'. A 35-year-old graduate is considered by academic standards an old wreck. I had already missed the bus, and all the possibilities to make a career. As someone confessed to me during an application process, my CV was instantly trashed, no matter what achievements I had listed in it, when the birth date was read.

So once again I renounced a career in physics. I lived for another six or seven years as a nomad, an academic scrap good for nothing, doing the most boring jobs, from giving private lessons, or reinventing myself again as popular science speaker, or becoming a programmer for psychology Ph.D. students (ironically doing for them what they were supposed to do, and permitting them to become what I had wanted to be, but could not). The cycle repeated itself, the story was already seen and lived. And yet my passion for science did not diminish. During these years I had several ideas in mathematical physics that were developed and even published in peer reviewed journals - nothing groundbreaking or revolutionary - but quite unusual stuff for someone who was supposed to be outside academia. I found myself doing a job I officially didn't have and yet dreamed of: doing research and publishing my findings. What a pity, though, that some journals don't publish if you don't have an affiliation, and when I asked some of my former professors about this, they refused to discuss the subject because of fear that they might be blamed by the faculty hierarchy. Eventually, after some clarifications, the articles were accepted.

But it became clear that this could not be my life. It makes no sense to live as an almost full-time researcher, to publish papers, and yet remain outside universities. Again my mind turned towards academia. What about a Ph.D.? At 42? Needless to say that the chances of success were extremely low. And, in fact, despite the several papers that had been published, and despite having shown myself to be fit in different areas of astrophysics, statistical mechanics, and mathematical physics, skills you will rarely find matured in young applicants, all attempts to enrol in a Ph.D. programme were rejected. I was too old. Period.

However, in one application, for six free doctoral-study positions, I ranked 12th out of 25. Well, just average, but not good enough. And yet destiny sometimes comes to one's rescue. The six aspirants before me left for one reason or another, and all of a sudden I found myself projected into a new world of sympathetic youngsters. *'I would have certainly preferred someone younger, but that's the law, I'm forced to accept you'*, was the warm welcome I received from my new Ph.D. advisor.

The time passed as a graduate student hadn't been that great either. Again I was forced to study a subject I wasn't interested in, silicon nanophotonics. However, being quite adaptable and flexible, I learned to enjoy it, but it was not the kind of study about the mysteries of nature and the cosmos that I was looking for. I told myself that it was still better than nothing. My dream to pursue a Ph.D. in physics had at last become a reality, and it would have been silly to throw away this opportunity.

So, while I dragged myself through another three years of study and research into something that I had not desired, one day I came across a book by Lee Smolin entitled *The Trouble with Physics* (9), which describes, in the second part, not only the scientific, but also the political, sociological and pedagogical reasons for failures in modern physical science. It was a flash of lightning and a revelation of something I deeply felt to be so true. It gave me an understanding of the profound uneasiness and dissatisfaction I always had with modern universities and with education in general. This gave me also the inner power to resist and go through the process of coming to terms with the realities affecting education. Perhaps, it was not cruel destiny, or a reflection of my weaknesses and inaptitude, but instead a pre-programmed path and process that had it as its object to mould me, shape me, and prepare me inwardly and psychologically and in character for something special. Several personal, lived experiences have shown me in the smallest of detail what education should *not* be. It slowly became crystal clear what the problem with education is. I began to understand the social dynamics and unconscious pedagogical and didactical processes which underlie learning in several schools and universities, that others find mysterious and puzzling, or are mostly not aware of. The book was certainly a catalyst, and a spark that lit a fire, but what I found most remarkable was the stark reality of having actually lived day after day what it described. It looked as if something wanted to show me the prevailing state of affairs in all its aspects and facets. Possibly this was not a coincidence.

These three years as a PhD student were particularly instructive. While I was not directly involved in industry, the working climate was pretty much influenced by that kind of mindset. The research I was involved in had only practical aims, it was of the kind an engineer might like to pursue (micro-resonant silicon optical circuits for future applications in the electronic industry), but certainly not something a theoretical physicist dreams of. My boss (aka 'advisor') was the typical authoritarian guy who believed that efficiency must equate with working under pressure in multitasking. However, I must give that experience credit for giving me a vision of a world I had not known before. The day of the doctoral thesis came. All went well.

Later I spent a year in France and another in Germany as a postdoc. But here again I found myself thrown into a working environment that did not furnish much intellectual perspective, and I felt like a fish out of water. I had to obey to the dictates of an industrialized hierarchical structure where everyone was only a little puppet that gets assigned a research task, the order in which it has to be executed, the method that must be employed, and obviously the deadline for it to be finished. Great discoveries in the history of science did not occur through the imposition of such a pre-programmed working style. But most of my colleagues were not at all dissatisfied, and considered such imposition of conditions a normal state of affairs. The ideal of the researcher who is free to think about a scientific project, and frees up his passion and creative potential making new experiments and discoveries in a laboratory, revealed itself only as a modern myth that has no grounds in reality, at least not for the vast majority of postdocs. The point is that after having gone through high school, graduated, worked through a Ph.D., what one is allowed to do as a postdoc is substantially to play the same game you were allowed to play in primary school! It is all the same system, the same matrix, but most adults delude themselves into believing that they are free. If the question arises what the alternative could be, they have no idea, and therefore think that after all they are lucky enough with what they have, with things as they are. It has always been so, why complain now?

But I don't blame anyone. I'm solely responsible for how things worked out for me. I didn't compromise, did not accept the status quo, felt uneasy where most of those who found themselves in a similar situation were perfectly happy. Obviously, it is something in my character and in my inner and emotional attitude that prevented me from breaking the barrier to become free. I don't want to make anyone responsible for my personal state of inner dissatisfaction. I consider the past a closed chapter, a remembrance for which I don't have regrets or bitterness (I once used to, but now I see it is futile). On the contrary, I realize today how it was a school of life that I had the honour to go through, and that gave me the possibility to enjoy extreme experiences that others rarely have. This made it possible to understand the state of affairs of our modern pedagogy, didactics, and their working environments, with exceptional clarity and depth of vision that, I believe, few have had an opportunity to enjoy. And what emerged from all that was a desire to focus in my coming years on an analysis of our present educational system, and a search for a real remedy for its shortcomings.

This led me to a dream. What I'm dreaming of is a new school, high school and university, a new concept and infrastructure which liberates the spirit and allows future generations to have what the present one is not allowed. The ideal for a new type of learning centres and a free academy came therefore from my dissatisfaction with the lack of time for contemplation outside the strict path put forward by the teacher's or professor's syllabus with no attempt to look beyond, for an intuitive and integral knowledge as I experienced it. I have been fully immersed in an environment where students are judged for the speed with which they graduate, the speed which they show in making calculations, and not for their aspiration and creativity. I was to discover that the instructor's capacity to change the system from within is strongly limited too by institutional demands and rules. Having experienced this state of affairs, I learnt at first hand, and with absolute clarity, just how decadent conventional education had become. Out of this experience grew a desire, a dream, to initiate something that would lead to giving the young generations the opportunities they still don't have. That became a persistent and enduring thought, and led me to reflect on new forms of education, learning, and free inner growth.

My experience as a school teacher

During my Ph.D. course, and especially during the few years working as a postdoc, I had to assist or teach university students. I then found myself on the other side of the lecture hall, and could see things from another perspective. Most of the students were quite skilled and smart minds, and yet I was appalled to see how ill equipped they were in developing a topic and conducting research on their own without someone telling them explicitly what to do, how to do it, and when to do it. This lack of passion, self-initiative, and desire to know more than what the official academic path proposes and implants in their minds, was quite revealing of how deep-seated the problem is. That problem may be traced back to the first years in ordinary schools, and eventually even to the kindergarten years. That is why I did not mind returning to the good old school system, where I worked as a teacher in a high school.

Therefore, the reason I decided to teach in a school was certainly not because of a propensity towards the ordinary school system. Even though I wanted to become a good teacher and convey as best as I could my knowledge and experience to young people, the real reason I embarked on this 'undercover mission' is summarized in the good old saying that *"to beat your enemy, you must know your enemy"*. And this not by reading books or developing an external theoretical understanding of how a system works but by working in it, experiencing and living it from the inside with all its plethora of problems, difficulties and challenges. Otherwise that would amount to what almost all professional academic pedagogues do: they lecture on how schools should work and on how children should learn but they have themselves never set a foot in a classroom as teachers.

I enrolled as a math and physics teacher in a Bavarian Waldorf school in Germany. A school inspired by the teachings of Rudolf Steiner, an Austrian philosopher, esotericist and educator, who in 1919 initiated a private school system that is quite common nowadays in Germany. Waldorf schools are very successful not only in Germany but have expanded, especially in the last decades, throughout the world. Since it is a school system based on alternative teaching methods and a different pedagogical concept than that of ordinary state schools, I naively believed I would find there an environment more open than elsewhere to libertarian and democratic perspectives on education. That was something which, as I was to learn soon, is light years away from reality. But first of all let me address shortly some positive aspects.

Steiner schools are rooted on quite controversial but, in some respects, interesting alternative pedagogical principles. The daily school practice directs its focus on subjects and activities which receive less emphasis than, or may even differ substantially from, those that children in ordinary schools find themselves exposed to. These principles and activities are based on Steiner's vision of the human being according to which we are more than a body with a brain, we are first and foremost spiritual beings with a much more complex structure. Besides the physical body, according to Steiner, as for many other spiritual traditions, there is also the 'astral body', the 'ethereal body' and the 'I'. The educational process must consider all these parts. That is, if it is to be true education, it should be education from the inside out, instead of the other way around, as most of us still tend to believe education should be. This esoteric teaching, which he used to call 'anthroposophy', attracted severe criticism from many sides, and remains one of the main reasons for its rejection by most pedagogues and by parents in search of an appropriate school for their children. I never embraced anthroposophy, and there are several aspects of his teachings which I would not subscribe to either. However, having myself a view of life and the universe as something which goes beyond matter, Steiner's spiritual approach never became for me a real ideological impediment, as it did for many other teachers (also Waldorf ones). Overall his expanded view of life beyond a material universe resonates with my own understanding of human nature and life.

Then again, the Waldorf pedagogy emphasizes the practical, and artistic development of pupils. Arts, music, painting, singing, carpentry, theatre and eurythmy (an expressive movement art originated by Steiner himself) characterize a typical Waldorf school workday. Even though this classroom structure comes to the detriment of more scientific and technical subjects, making my life as a science teacher not any easier, I have in principle no objection to the approach. If children prefer playing a musical instrument or making a theatre play than studying mathematics, they get all my sympathy.

Also, the phenomenological approach to science taught in Waldorf schools, with its stress on intuition and the qualitative experience, besides the strict intellectual, empirical, reductionist and quantitative approach of ordinary science, has potential to become a basis for future science.

Of great value in my view are the typical Waldorf 'main lesson blocks' ('Epochenunterricht'), a term which subsumes a subject lesson or topic that is taught daily (typically for 100 to 120 minutes) and intensively for a period of three or four weeks. During this period of time pupils show their ability to learn much better, and concentrate a great deal on a wide variety of subject matter that lies beyond traditional curricula.

Moreover, in Waldorf schools pupils in the 8th and 11th grades have to prepare annual projects of their choice. This offers a great opportunity for a practical and intellectual self-unfoldment, an opportunity I could only have dreamt of in my youth.

This scheme recently evolved into a proposal (an idea which however seems to remain frozen in an eternal 'experimental phase'), for the introduction of portfolios, a development that the FPE community heartily welcomes. There will be no grades to award, except for the last two years in the case of those preparing for the external state exams. Poor performance by a pupil will not force him or her to repeat their class. The resulting freedom from pressure can only be welcome where previously there were anxiety and burnouts. Not all problems and illnesses disappear, though, as I will make clear shortly. At the same time, there is value in Steiner's pedagogical approach, and several practices associated with it could be found useful in other similar contexts.

However, I was soon to discover the other side of the coin. As is often the case, the worst enemy of our ideals and noble intentions turns out to be ourselves. In my opinion and according to my experience, it is the Waldorf school system itself which is intrinsically unsuited for Steiner's pedagogical concepts. Steiner dreamt of freedom of culture, freedom of education, equality and fraternity. His schools should have been the foundation stone for this 'threefold social order'. Waldorf schools are perhaps a place where children can and practise equality and fraternity better than in ordinary schools. But the very same school system he himself sanctioned is in striking contrast with his own ideals of freedom. As regards the freedoms, Waldorf schools are just like any ordinary state or private schools. Pupils are forced five to eight hours a day to attend lessons, teacher-centred instruction remains the dominant teaching paradigm, obligation for all to attend at all times remains an unquestioned rule, a strict organization into grades and classrooms according to age is inescapable, and the freedom to express one's own potentialities by opting for a subject instead of another is in most cases not allowed. A false concept of community and unity dominates, and everyone has to do with all the others the same things at the same time and in the same manner. Despite claims to the contrary, my experience showed me how Waldorf schools are not particularly original: at the centre stands the collective, while the individual remains a marginal figure who must follow and obey. Then this is called a 'comprehensive school'.

In principle, teachers have freedom of teaching what and how they desire. Officially there is a Waldorf curriculum for every subject and grade, but it is more of an indication and help than a strict plan to follow. This freedom is to some degree realized, especially in the primary and secondary school, since the final state exams are still far away. In high school, however, where this time is nearing, students as well as teachers must conform to the upper directives of a system they later will need to be recognized from. In the typical Waldorf 'main lessons block', there is still some freedom to teach different subjects and to apply original teaching and learning formats. However, since the maths training of an average Waldorf high school student is behind that of those of an ordinary state school of a couple of years, a maths teacher isn't left with much time to address topics which are not in line with the state curriculum.

While one cannot make Steiner and his followers responsible for this (the state's sword of Damocles with its examination is an issue every private school must confront), the main issue I faced as a teacher and one that literally tortured me during these years (in contrast to most of my colleagues) was: aside from the question of the finals, can there be any freedom of teaching at all if there is no freedom to learn? After having tried every possible didactical and pedagogical instrument I had access to, my answer is a definite 'No!' For most teachers, it is a quite normal state of affairs that children do not want to go to school, and hate learning. They enjoy teaching regardless of what their pupils think and feel. But I didn't want to blind myself, and came to the conclusion that there can be no joy in teaching if there is no joy in learning. Only if one side is free to learn and enjoys the pleasure of discovery can the other side be said to be really free to teach and manifest an ability as instructor. So, my sober conclusion is that the fatal error of Steiner was to cling to a system made of the very same substance, namely compulsions and psychological pressures on children, which characterizes the state system he wanted to distance his system from, and yet was supposed to produce free culture and free thinking people for a new social order. One might even say that Steiner's pedagogy never came into life in its full potentiality, since it was suffocated at birth by Waldorf schools.

The real issue for me was to test how far my own abilities as instructor could go, where the cognitive skills of youngsters stood, what the real happenings behind the official scene are, and how I could eventually enhance the effectiveness of working from the inside of a private but nevertheless quite conventional structure. It was not my object to verify a particular pedagogical theory or the educational effectiveness of a school.

The impact was for me emotionally devastating. Unfortunately, most of my suspicions and fears about how detrimental and negative school is for the psyche of children were only confirmed and strengthened. I could directly observe how our schools impair their cognitive abilities reducing them to passive and subservient slaves.

Let me first describe my experience with young people attending high school classes in math and physics. I will not go into the details of their mathematical skills, which were very poor and ill developed (since this might be due to the lack of proper preparation, a problem specific to Waldorf schools). What was much more depressing was not only the low technical skills level of the young children, but especially their frustration, lack of interests, passivity and absence of goals in life as well as an inability to look beyond the given schemes. In principle, all schools underline their efforts to involve young people into a learning process which is supposed to foster their passion, individual potentials, curiosity and originality. Generations of teachers devolved their lives to this aim, but not with much success, from what I could see. Some critics complain about good textbooks and proper educational material. But that isn't the case. If a teacher looks up carefully the literature one finds also excellent readings. It became obvious for me how a system which is centred on a forced classroom attendance inevitably severely hampers the development of a child in the first place, whatever pedagogical approach and means we set in place. We first prescribe what children have to learn, pack them tightly several hours a day in a classroom and only rarely allow them to learn what they want to and then wonder why, after a decade of forced intellectual labour, so few nurture interests that go beyond who is at the top of the last hit-parade or what the tabloid hero in fashion is actually doing, but do not know at all what they want from life.

My attempts to motivate them were not entirely unsuccessful. In fact, one can indeed emotionally and mentally involve a third of the class by introducing subjects which go beyond a formal dryness. For example, in maths that could be problems which involve practical aspects of life, the beauty of geometrical structures, or the emergence of mathematical laws in nature. In physics the teacher might let them perform experiments, report about the life of scientists of the past, or show them interesting documentaries. Yes, there are methods which make lessons more alive and interesting, but if a teacher sincerely looks at the faces and the expressions of the pupils in the classroom who must do their tasks, fascinating as these might be, he or she could not miss the fact that they are not passionate, they are just a bit more willing to cooperate. And this was not what I was looking for.

What came through as particularly striking for me was the severe lack of resilience in the students. Most simply gave up at their very first encounter with a difficulty. Any cognitive exercise which could not be executed immediately by a mechanical procedure was set aside. An inquisitive learning approach was far beyond their imagination. This became very clear in the so called 'weak students'. In a culture that does not allow for failures and errors, they were forced to accumulate year after year so many negative experiences that something broke inside, and any attempt to solve a problem which needs a conscious effort beyond a 30-second time interval, recalled in their minds frustrating feelings. An internal automatism opted to quit. In maths, this is particularly detrimental since this is inherently a discipline which needs resilient error-tolerant learning where failure is just a step of the learning process, not the ultimate decree about one's own abilities. But it is hard to make this clear to someone who has been taught always the contrary. I had to lead to their final exam several students who couldn't even perform the simplest algebraic calculations. The hardest thing for me as instructor wasn't that I had to cover the huge amount of maths lessons left behind untouched by many teachers. It was to convince them that their problem was not a matter of intelligence or inborn skills, but that it was one of self-esteem lost in years of frustrations and negative experiences.

In this frame, things become even worse when one does not know what freedom is. Young minds who never experienced real free learning conditions since childhood become unable to control and discipline themselves if at an older age they are suddenly left free to do what they want. If real freedom is allowed, the chances that it will break out into chaos or an inert passivity are very high. This is not just a theory or a speculation, but a fact I could test on the ground myself. For example, as a teacher I frequently used to propose several topics to investigate, and students had to prepare a presentation. They also had the option to choose freely a topic of their own interest. Almost none did (about an average of one or two on twenty), none of the others felt confident enough to go their own way and interests.

Lack of freedom leads also to undisciplined behaviour once freedom is allowed. Because authoritarianism leads to a false understanding of what freedom is. When asked what freedom is about, most will say: 'It is the right to do whatever we want to'. What remains unexpressed, but is unconsciously present in this interpretation, is that one is eventually also free to harm others. In the understanding of most of these children, who were raised in a conventional school, there is no connection between freedom and responsibility. In fact, quite the contrary tends to prevail: freedom is seen also as freedom from any responsibility and self-restraint. A teacher who allows children to be completely free to do what they want may become quickly a helpless observer of how the class spirals into a total chaos, eventually also degenerating in physical damage and threat to objects and persons. On one occasion I could verify this myself: apart from shouting and pushing up the noise levels, some children began to play with their lighters trying to set paper and curtains on fire. I had to interrupt the 'experiment' (too late—paper planes in flames had already taken off from the windows). But this didn't come as a surprise to me. It is a quite logical consequence of an authoritarian concept of education. Children who are limited in their freedom to express themselves are also not allowed to practise responsible behaviour for their free actions. They simply don't understand what that could mean. Self-discipline, responsibility and respect for others remain empty words. It is an inherent contradiction of our school system that we pretend from them responsibility, but at the same time accurately prevented them to learn it from the outset. What we urgently need instead are schools where freedom AND responsibility are practised at the same time.

Of course, this does not apply to all. There are also several children and students who attend school, perform well, act responsibly and even like it. Many talk about their life from primary school to high school as a happy time. But in these cases one wonders if they would say the same thing if they had had the opportunity to compare their experience with an alternative that would have shown them how education could be lived also otherwise.

Overall my impression was nevertheless that of a generation asking for a meaning and purpose. Without rationalizing and verbalizing it directly, I always had the net impression that especially the grown-ups were constantly struggling for a meaning but could find none. The entire school system, as it exists today, has become a heavy and meaningless burden, and the grown-ups find it hard to explain why they find themselves in it. The only thing that prevents them from giving up is that piece of paper, a certificate, that would eventually allow them to find a job. Extrinsic motivation points at a material and economic purpose but nothing encourages the child to build upon a purpose of inner self-realization.

There is also the lack of alternatives to the current school system. If one quits, what then? Is there an alternative route to these certificates and jobs?

In fact there are several, but these require self-discipline and the ability to practise a self-determined learning, which is precisely what they have been robbed of from the outset at their early stages in school. So the problem becomes circular. A genius must have invented this enslavement matrix!

Another aspect which I felt was very limiting was the lack of freedom of teachers themselves. Besides the conventional obligations of a teacher (preparing lessons, writing and correcting tests, re-writing and re-correcting new ones for a second term, attending parents-teacher conferences, being always ready to jump in for replacement lessons, writing school certificates, attending training seminars, just to mention few examples), was the permanent pressure to arrange mountains of internal bureaucratic matters, the obligation to attend endless conferences where everything is discussed except those issues one feels are necessary and useful, the organization and compulsory participation in any sort of celebrations, attending meetings where any kind of emergency had to be sorted out, etc., etc. While these kinds of problems notoriously plague state and private schools, they are however particularly acute in Waldorf schools for two reasons. First, the common explanation is that since there is no official hierarchy, what in a conventional school is quickly decided by a principal in a Steinerian school has to undergo throughout a long decisional process before action is taken in the framework of a common democratic consensus. But in my opinion this reflects only a partial truth and does not go to the roots of the problem. The second and most burdensome cause is again this false idea of unity in uniformity, which also forces teachers and youngsters alike into common dry and colourless tasks and assignments.

What really blocks the self-expression of many instructors is a false understanding of a collective unity which is supposed to glue very different personalities into a community, in this case a group of teachers. The fiction which is hard to get rid of in our current mindset is that the members of a healthy community must work all together on the same projects and problems at the same time. It is this idea which envisages an organization as a group of people, all of them doing the same thing at the same time and in the same manner. It is this tendency to believe that all administrative work, the issues related to the internal organization and the initiatives of a school must all be worked out by everyone, independently of their interests and skills. However, this is not unity, but a pale and flattened form of uniformity without a real energy behind it (an issue I will touch upon again later because it becomes central in the decision-making process of an FPE structure).

The school system is becoming an increasingly complex endeavour. As the years passed by, I could see mountains of obligations accumulate, and lots of issues emerge that were previously of little or no importance. Most teachers are busy with such a huge amount of organizational and internal procedures to manage that there is virtually no time, and especially no vital energy left, to implement new forms of teaching. Those teachers that take their job seriously and work full time frequently, sooner or later, manifest symptoms of burnout. Fatigue and permanent exhaustion, if prolonged over the years, inevitably leads to a nervous breakdown. I could mention several cases of colleagues who had to leave because of a burnout syndrome, I had to cut my teaching load myself to avoid this trap. Generally, at least in the school environment I worked in, one could sense an atmosphere of nervous tension and permanent apprehension in most of my colleagues. Teachers revealed their inner and physical distress among themselves with irritation, and sometimes hysterical outbursts towards other colleagues. A tiny misunderstanding or mistake could cause uncontrolled emotional reactions which led to prolonged conflicts and heated quarrels. That was something very far from the kind of sense of community and social unity one was supposed to build, represent, and maintain. My depiction of what I have seen present-day schools become might sound too negative an account of a reality that, after all, has worked well for centuries and that at any rate has given birth to our modern materially well-developed society. Were it not for schools, humanity would be still living in the Middle Ages. And, of course, several counterexamples of young creative and imaginative intellects come to mind too. And yes, not everything in that institution we call 'school' turned out to be so negative. However, the average cognitive level, but especially the ability to self-determine their tasks and self-direct their work, that I found in most children and teenagers was quite disappointing. Moreover, the organizational structure on which schools are built is a motivation-killing machine that only rarely allows for individual self-development and self-unfoldment in students and teachers alike.

I know that several, if not most of my colleagues, would disagree with this harshly negative verdict. *'In my classroom children are enthusiastic'*, or *'You can have an effect and change a lot also inside the given school context'*, might be typical replies one should expect to hear. During my first term as a novice educator, I tended to interpret the discrepancy between what I could see in the classrooms and what other colleagues told me about their experience as something coming from my inexperience as teacher. In fact, these years as a pedagogue contributed enormously in increasing my skills, knowledge and understanding of how things work in a school system and what transforms an inexperienced teacher into an average instructor. But the undeniable fact that I had to deal with every day, that of a lost generation which acts like many (undisciplined) soldiers, most of them utterly unwilling to go beyond a pre-ordered curriculum and waiting for orders (frequently unattended) from a more or less authoritarian figure who is supposed to tell them what is right and what is wrong, never left me. It only crystallized. I came to the conclusion that also those teachers who are considered the best and most experienced ones (I do not put myself in this category) and who boast about their achievements in the classroom, are only telling themselves fairy tales. In our society, we are so accustomed to the idea that kids naturally dislike to go to school, they aren't willing to learn, that sitting six to eight hours a day or more on a chair behind a table absorbing all the time dry notions and concepts, is an inevitable malady that we all have to go through and that we no longer even question. It is this attitude that blinds us and prevents us from realizing the miserable state of the mental and emotional health of our youth. One treats as normal sleepy and frustrated faces in the classroom, attempts to avoid lessons, cheating during tests, expressing hate and resentment against one or more subjects, undisciplined behaviours, boredom, lack of initiative and of curiosity, or a passive reception of notions without an interest to go beyond a sterile learning scheme. The unexpressed ever-present unconscious thought that lingers in the background is that this is how things always have been, it is already the best that can exist. Children must be forced to learn because, so goes the theory, they are not able to self-direct their learning, and that this dissatisfaction and inertia in schools is something we must accept as a normal daily fact. And if sometimes a teacher is skilled enough to boost the morale beyond this average state of affairs, then he can proudly tell others how motivated and happy his students are. After all, how can someone admit that in one's own decade-long career there might be something fundamentally archaic and wrong? But this does not change the fact that it is a self-delusion. A running in a hamster-wheel where the hamster refuses to acknowledge the wheel itself believing it is a highway to the future. A deception we willingly submit to because we don't know how things could be otherwise. Just a nice story whose function is first of all to deny oneself in order to acknowledge the painful reality, how we are all not much more than little cogs in a big machine that crunches everything that longs for individuality and change.

During the years that I actively worked as a teacher, I could observe and live in myself as an 'empath' who feels the energies in a classroom the suffering and the distress of many children and youngsters. Clinical depression, suicidal thoughts, bulimia, anorexia, ADD and ADHD (whatever that might be, or not be), mental illnesses of all sorts, etc., are rampant in our modern society, and schools are making it only worse.

Boredom and a lack of interest were also visible in most of the others. However, boredom should always be interpreted as signifying a lack of inner growth. This is precisely what should encourage adults to create an environment where this growth can take place. The almost unanimous and facile explanation is: *'It's because of TV or too many computer games or an addiction to smartphones.'* I'm quite critical of the use of new media amongst children, but when this becomes a mono-causal explanation, it sounds more like an excuse to avoid seeking the root causes of the symptoms that one is trying to explain. Unfortunately, these symptoms are only the tip of an iceberg and are destined to become worse and more widespread if we continue to ignore reality and put our heads in the sand. School in its conventional structure is no longer working. We can reform, restructure, amend or ameliorate it also for another trillion times, but that won't change anything much. All the innumerable reforms of the past two centuries didn't either. School is in its essence and core outdated and is ruining our youth. If we want to perpetuate a social structure which is made of obedient but ignorant and unreflective little ants, school as it is is just fine. But if we would like to go only a little bit beyond this state of affairs, school in its core concept must be reconsidered and most of it abolished entirely.

I believe that every teacher who shares these ideas and opinions on the current school system should resign and look for another job. What is the point of serving an institution which harms the individual as also the collective well-being? Why should someone continue to support an organization if it is seen as perpetrating a sort of 'institutionalized child abuse'? In fact, that is precisely what I did. After three years of teaching experience, I quit my job.

Increasingly, I have become aware of how school is an institution that can no longer be reformed, and how that is no longer compatible with my conscience. A profession which, in this form, is pointless and only serves to maintain an ancient and rotten system that makes young people sick and stupid. I cannot and do not want to participate any longer.

I've gone through the entire educational spectrum from bottom to top: primary and secondary education, going through my 'Abitur' (German secondary level exam), then with graduation in university, later made my PhD, then worked as a research associate in research centres in Italy, shortly in France, then in Germany and, finally, returned to school. I have seen the educational system from all sides as a pupil, student, doctorand, postdoc researcher, and then as a teacher. So, I know very well from direct experience what I'm talking about when I say, for example, that the day will come when we will look back and realize how schools can be compared to child labour in coal mines.

As long as we do not fundamentally rethink the system, the structure, and the framework, school will become—especially for the coming generations—increasingly an experience of frustration and a psychological impoverishment. We can reform as much as we wish; train and pay teachers better; build new schools; introduce other laws; and create great novel educational approaches, but none of this will help much in the long term. One can train the prison guards well, but the prisoners will still not be happy and free citizens. Discontent towards the school system can only grow steadily.

In part, I already knew what would have come up to me when I returned to school, but I wanted to return and immerse myself into the "school matrix", to live it again from the inside perspective of the educator down to its abysses. In this respect, without doubt, one could certainly say "mission accomplished", but not without having gone through a strong dose of frustration and defeat to the brink of depression and burnout.

What I learned, experienced, and understood is actually immense. This became clear to me only today. It formed, shaped, and 'educated' me, leading me to a lot of self-reflection and, at the same time, making me grow inwardly. In general, thanks to this direct experience of the last three decades, I could write tomes, not only about how today's education works internally or externally, or what does not work in our education system, but also, more importantly, how it subtly and subliminally conditions the subconscious of children, adolescents, and adults, and how it very skilfully turns off our will power. A reprogramming on the part of the *Matrix*, which manipulates us through instinctual thought patterns and, above all, keeps us under control with fear, like puppets. The film is much more realistic than what we might think. I always assert that not money but fear governs the world. This was partly clear to me, but was realized fully only through my experience in the teaching profession.

There is a nice saying: "Being a teacher is not a profession, but a call and a vocation". Yes, I can confirm this.

But a call and vocation to do what?

A vocation to force yourself in order to force others.

A vocation to force children to do something that is NOT their vocation.

A vocation to brag about self-determination, creativity, and the great mood of the school, without being aware that one is only telling himself a fairy tale.

A vocation to prepare each day the stuff students must be trained with, without having to worry about whether they really care or not.

A vocation to stubbornly ignore countless scientific studies of recent decades with evidence that demonstrates how our notions of school education are completely out of place.

A vocation to believe that children learn nothing without compulsion and that they are not able to take self-responsibility without pressure.

A vocation not to question anything and to belittle student's questions (mostly unconsciously, without even realizing it).

A vocation to express an (authoritarian) authority and leadership that aims to keep the class "under control" (according to the motto "I myself learned it that way...").

A vocation to participate at interminable teacher conferences where only very few really want to attend because of the infinite bureaucratic issues that hardly allow one to tackle pedagogically relevant topics (and even when this happens, the existing pedagogical paradigm is never questioned anyway).

A vocation to be ultimately unaware of how one is just a slave of the system and, quite to the contrary, enjoying it by a perfect adaptation to it.

No, I'm not a good teacher because I do not have this vocation and call. So, it was time to give it up and go....

Thanks to these experiences, however, I became not only aware of how the medieval system we call 'school' is by far no longer up-to-date and that it should be abolished, but also how home- and un-schooling in the present form (about which I will go into deeper in a coming chapter) are only precursors to a new form of education of free, self-determined development that still doesn't exists but, even though only from the far, is now becoming visible to me.

In the course of time, an idea took shape that did not envisage just "new" or "democratic" schools or institutions. A vision of large, compulsive-free, self-educational learning places that do not require any obligatory presence but that are available infrastructurally. Free learning environments where everyone can join and leave without restrictions, where everyone can learn what is interesting to oneself, and where one can determine his own learning-path, without time pressure or compulsory curriculum.

I do not regret anything and would do everything again to go through this experience to reach this awareness. But there is no way back either. I will never be a school teacher again!

The problem with modern education

The spell of utilitarianism in the industrial era and the decline of science

A reflection on my life, which I have described, right from my school years to my recent experience as a high-school teacher, prompted me to give thought to the root causes of the malaise that afflicts modern education. Why is it that not all of the innumerable reforms and changes and revisions have brought so little real or significant improvement in the centuries-old education system of ours? In the best of cases, they have barely scratched the surface of the system's problems. Even those who hold conservative views on the subject have been expressing their dissatisfaction with the present state of affairs, and are now voicing a demand for fundamental revisions in the structure of the educational system.

There are several different possible approaches to analyse the deep reasons that lie behind the crisis of present-day education. One is to analyse first the historical development of education science.

The first schools and structured university-like educational systems appeared as early as the 6th century AD under the aegis of the Latin Church in monastic schools in which monks and nuns taught classes. The first learning environment awarding degrees, and autonomous from religious authority, was the University of Bologna in 1088, a law school. However, the impulse to build these institutions didn't come from purely practical considerations, but resulted also from the renewed interest in philosophy and natural philosophy gained from the rediscovery of the ancient Greek texts. Besides arithmetic and geometry, law and medicine, academic fields that were not really the most practical and financially profitable academic topics, such as metaphysics, music, and astronomy, can be considered the oldest subjects of study that humanity pursued. The rediscovery of the ancient Greek works, in particular those of Aristotle, ignited an intellectual effort that was directed primarily towards an understanding of the natural world and its processes, a spirit of inquiry that had no necessity for direct or immediate practical applications. And, interestingly enough, most medieval universities were based on a free student-controlled organization.

This changed only later, about five centuries after the first Bologna university, with the emergence of the nation-state, which brought education under state control, whereby a centralized organization and the faculty governance model was introduced. It is in this context of universities increasingly under a centralized authoritarian and hierarchical control that the cultural stagnation, unable to disengage itself from the Aristotelian worldview, and which led to the well-known resistance against the emergence of the scientific revolution, became prominent and particularly acute. As the case of Galileo showed eloquently, it was not this kind of institution (we still have some of them around, even though no longer under religious control), but the spirit, originality, brilliance, and stubbornness of the individual against this power structure that could change the cultural landscape.

It was not before the beginning of the 20th century that education opened itself to the masses. The First World War was around the corner, and the Industrial Revolution had already transformed the human condition. The emphasis on practical sciences such as engineering was unavoidable. While the modern roots of industrial efficiency can be traced back to the Industrial Revolution, its scientific systematization is owed to Winslow Taylor (1856–1915), an American mechanical engineer and father of 'scientific management'. In his view, every stage of workflow has to conform to precise stipulated processes. In American industries, everything had to be done according to scientifically preconceived plans that tell workers what was to be done, how it was to be done, and when it was to be done. In this view, the potential of the individual has no value. The individual has only to follow the preordered set of duties imparted from above by a hierarchy which is itself subordinate to the principles of scientific management. And, of course, everything and everyone is permanently monitored and evaluated for quality and efficiency. Taylor's theories, consciously or unconsciously, became quickly the working paradigm of the early 20th century, especially in the war industry. The best caricature of this state of affairs was Charlie Chaplin's 1936 film 'Modern Times'.

Nowadays, officially, no manager, politician, or teacher takes Taylorism seriously. Officially. But this concept, which envisages a vast and concentrated effort of pre-indoctrinated human resources that follow orders towards a unique goal, and necessarily organizes, predicts, and pre-orders tightly each one's duties, remains a deeply engraved mindset and modus operandi. It is a trend that tries forcefully to replace the free autonomous thinker with a businessman–corporate type professional figure at all levels. The administration, which organizes and directs from a hierarchical authority a priori everyone's path, study, research, and duties, is rooted in a mindset in which management positions with corporate experience are praised, and which look to the original outsider thinker as a little brother or soldier that has to be controlled and directed from above. And since this approach had proven itself to be very effective in mass production, not least the mass production of weapons that bolstered the two world wars, and has been doing the same for modern warfare, it has been assumed for a long time that this would equally help bring about enhanced productivity and success in the realm of education. The idea to transfer and generalize a purely utilitarian management model from industry to other human activities is unfortunately a malady that continues to plague our modern culture, and reflects itself in the tendency to create assembly-line schools.

And, as would be true of any assembly line, it must be predictable system. In fact, the compulsive need for predictability is another distinctive characteristic of modern managerial thinking, which it usually terms euphemistically as 'accountability', and that spread its tentacles into schools, and even into higher education. The outcome of a research project, the properties of a product, the time to develop it, its quality and function, and the length of time it would a student to acquire knowledge and skills are the elements required to be precisely planned and predicted in advance. And by doing so, the obsession with business plans and 'technology roadmaps' dominates the industrial and now also the educational world. Alongside those elements, there must also be predictable application potential for every research project. Increasingly unlikely to be approved and sponsored are fundamental science projects that aim at gaining mere theoretical knowledge, but do not explicitly indicate an outcome that is supposed to lead to a practical application, or at least guarantee the achievement of a goal set in advance.

This is in striking contrast to historical experience that showed how all too often the goal and the possible applications of a study and the usefulness of a research project become clear, not at its conception, but during the process, and frequently also long after its completion. What is killed along the way is the process of creative and spontaneous development of the project itself, which remains forced inside a small, preordered human mind map. Any attempt to expunge the unpredictable factor, and refuse to allow space to alternative goals and direction readjustments along the research path, is against any historical experience. Several great human advancements became possible because of coincidences and sudden, unexpected discoveries.

What if Christopher Columbus, whose goal was to discover India, having sighted the coast of America, had decided to sail back since this was not in line with his 'roadmap'? Ridiculous as it may sound, this is precisely how the modern, tightly fixed delimitations and boundary conditions in the modern research flow work. They impede the unexpected, and hamper human originality and the spirit of personal initiative. An attitude such as this, which wants to predict everything, comes also from the historic success of Galilean and Newtonian science itself, where the prediction and control of the fundamental mechanical behaviour of particles and bodies, and the construction of machines, led to the explosive development of technology. Instinctively, therefore, we maintain to this day this unconscious attitude that wants to predict the human's behaviour and the mind's productivity, equating them to a mechanical phenomenon, and believing that this might emulate the technological success of the past. No wonder that entrepreneurs lament a crisis of creative, independent, original thinking, since these are aspects of the human mind and spirit, which will always remain essentially unpredictable in outcome, extent, and time. They ask for flexibility when they fixed at the outset a scarcely flexible path themselves.

What makes things worse is that this mindset is vitiated by a sort of 'utilitarian spell' that hypnotizes even the smartest minds, according to which nothing is of value if its practical application isn't already clear from the outset. This is a spell that inflicts a great deal of suffering especially on the pure science sector (with few notable exceptions like particle physics or space exploration), but that is against all historical evidence. The recent trend in many schools and among several teachers is that to teach mathematics only if backed by its applications in the real world. The rationale behind this idea is that practical applications of a discipline which is intrinsically based on abstractions and that much too often is lived with aversion and frustration, is supposed to become more attractive if children can relate it to the real world. Any experienced pedagogue who tried this out knows, however, that this theory is flawed. An intellectual link to practice alone will not make things more interesting, whereas it is the living experience to set themselves into the flow, to discover one's ability to concentrate and especially the pleasure of understanding, and having an insight and realization of a mathematical structure or a law, which really sparks interest towards an abstract discipline like maths. People, from childhood to advanced age enjoy music, theatre plays, films, poetry, painting, and all sorts of arts. But nobody asks what their practical applications are supposed to be. We enjoy these things for they awaken something in us that is not necessarily connected to a utilitarian outcome. There is no reason to believe that for maths things should be otherwise. Most mathematicians and scientists did not opt for their career because of a desire to find applications. If Kepler, Galileo or Newton had this attitude, modern science couldn't have been born (and, by the way, the 'practical' application Newton had in mind, if any, was alchemy). If Planck, Einstein, and many others had thought only of the practical application of their theories, neither relativity nor quantum mechanics would exist. Many applied sciences today are actually based on the discoveries of people who did not have applications in mind. They pursued knowledge for its own sake, and found it by and in themselves on the basis of what the knowledge current at their time allowed them to do.

This utilitarian mindset that reigns in modern academic environments permits little freedom to personal skills, creative, original thought, and productive power to express themselves. Of course, there are no written laws that forbid independence of thought, and, quite to the contrary, all too many praise themselves for being 'free' and 'independent'. Yet the intolerance of creativity and questioning manifest indirectly, in a more subtle way, but very systematically and efficiently. If you are one of those who dream of understanding the logic of nature by following their intrinsic motivation and creative spirit of inquiry through an intellectual, independent process, you are almost certain to have a hard time in a standard school or academic institution which places all its efforts, not on an individualized form of learning, but on an indoctrinating path strewn with tests and selections.

At university, if your line of research is not in line with mainstream research or the most accepted trend, and which usually are those which receive almost exclusively all the funds, you won't be able to make your way through modern research centres. If you want to graduate listening to your inner call by following a path of your own, as an undergraduate, you will soon be disappointed: you are usually not allowed to follow the studies you feel more appropriate for yourself. As a graduate, you rarely will find an advisor or tutor asking what your call is, and, as a researcher, you will rarely be able to find someone hiring you in doing an original, non-mainstream research. Even as a top manager directing a large research centre, you will be highly dependent on a funding policy which usually does not allow for a research that goes off-track. Finally, almost all efforts are devoted to learning how to 'play the game'. This is, obviously, in striking contrast to what the word 'education' means. It comes from the Latin 'educere', which means 'to draw out' or the 'pulling forward' of wisdom from within. The word 'school' comes from the Greek word σχολή (skholē), which surprisingly means 'leisure', 'spare time', and only later became 'philosophy' or 'lecture place'. It is interesting to note how the etymology of our everyday language seems to retain a breath of ancient wisdom that we have lost, but now desperately need to recover. In a world where a mechanical learning system is focused on ramming abstract notions into young brains, there is no longer any education, but only an 'inducation'.

Physics Nobel laureate Peter Higgs, credited for his theoretical discovery of the particle named after him, the Higgs boson, admitted that, according to present-day academic logic, he 'wouldn't be productive enough'. (10) At the time of his discovery, he did not have to his credit a sufficient number of publications even to be hired, and nowadays he would not be allowed to have sufficient time to concentrate on the theories that led him to his findings. In fact, one rule of this game is the well known 'publish or perish' rule, with institutional pressure for lots of papers to be published in so called 'high-impact' journals. Not without deleterious side effects. The belief in using journal rank as an assessment tool turns out to be bad scientific practice. (11) Paradoxically, the negative effects of institutionalizing journal rank could be observed in the increase in the number of incorrect or inaccurate scientific published claims, which led to a sharp increase in the retraction rate of articles published in scientific journals from the early 2000s on. The level of evidence-based claims and the reproducibility of experiments, which is the very basis of any Galilean and Newtonian scientific methodology, declined as well. Journal rank is a poor indicator of methodological soundness. Furthermore, an interesting analysis showed what kind of negative and ridiculous consequences the 'publish or perish' rule created in the last four decades. (12) Researchers at the University Medical Center Utrecht in the Netherlands showed how the frequency of positive-sounding words such as 'novel', 'amazing', 'innovative' and 'unprecedented' increased almost nine-fold in titles and abstracts of research papers published between 1974 and 2014. This increase in hype and the exaggeration of novelty and the potential for breakthrough with which scientists present their research shows an increasing and almost obsessive need to attract attention and over-emphasize one's own research when one should instead be presenting sober facts without resorting to emotional wordings. With this academic research approach, those who publish fewer but qualitatively better research papers tend to be ignored, while those who produce a large number of low-level and over-hyped papers get much more attention. The result is that good and honest research is penalized while bad science, by getting into the media headlines much more easily, is consequently also much more funded.

This unwritten 'publish-or-perish' rule that permeates modern academia was not unnoticed by publishing companies eager to make a business out of it. Particularly alarming is the phenomenon of so-called 'predatory journals' – that is, open-access academic publishing services that charge publication fees for the flood of papers coming worldwide from authors in dire need of publishing as much as possible, but without, or only scarcely, providing a serious peer review and editing service. Skipping the peer review and editing phase allows authors to make an impact by quickly releasing several papers which, however, lack professional scrutiny. The point is that most scientists are not aware that they are being lured into a dishonest practice, as the journal falsifies the evaluation of their work (hence, the name 'predatory'). This fraudulent business model is not limited to a few journals. Beall's list of predatory journals and publishers includes hundreds of questionable online scholarly open-access journals! (13) This overall state of affairs has led to a decline in the quality of science. The scientists who survive and have successful careers are not those who have the best skills and expertise, but those who are able to sell themselves and their work, not rarely by dubious and questionable means.

Jeffrey C. Hall, an American geneticist and chronobiologist who was awarded the 2017 Nobel Prize in physiology or medicine for the discovery of molecular mechanisms controlling the circadian rhythm, was adamantly clear about how research institutions no longer employ researchers but exploit them as 'scriptwriter' for scientific journals. *"There is huge pressure on the overworked, anxious AI (Actual Investigators) to bring something 'great' to the boss, who wants everything to go to a vanity journal."* - *"What props up biological research, at least in the vaunted US of A, involves a situation so deeply imbued with entitlement mentality that it has sunk into institutional corruption. A principal symptom of this state of affairs involves the following: People are hired after they have undergone long stints of training; and a potential hiree must present a large body of documented accomplishments. In my day you could get a faculty job with zero post-doc papers, as in the case of yours truly; but now the CV of a successful applicant looks like that of a newly minted full Professor from olden times."* (14)

Anyone who asks for time to focus on a topic, especially if it challenges the established assumptions, might get sympathetic comments like 'Your line of research is quite interesting, but ...'. However, anyone who persists in this stance will have to struggle hard to get a job, and will have no chance to get a permanent position. Another Nobel Laureate, Randy Schekman, declared that he would no longer publish in 'luxury journals', such as Nature or Cell and Science, in protest against the 'tyranny of the impact factor' which 'distorts the scientific process'. (15)

Schekman's statements reminds me of the fact that it is not only the individual's but also the institute's prestige and standing that counts over everything else (which is frequently linked, among other things, to absurd international university rankings based on obsessive quantifications of unmeasurable qualities), and how it frequently leads to acts of self-censorship by the institute against its own staff. If someone proposes an original idea, a new idea which, however, is not mainstream or is controversial, in most academic institutions, a mechanism of immediate internal reprimand may come into action. What counts first and foremost is the academy's reputation, prestige, and name in the external world. A whole set of centralized, unwritten regulations come into force, typically refusing affiliation. While this is understandable from the point of view of a department that has to preserve its stature and approval, especially in the eyes of the external funding institutions, it has frequently become a factor for inhibition and suppression of novel schemes, creative potentials, and fresh ideas only because they are not in line with the current and dominant thought.

Thomas Sinkjær, former director of the Danish National Research Foundation in Copenhagen, interviewed 400 young scientists and reports how he *"kept hearing the same depressing refrain: many were writing grants not for work they really wanted to do, but for projects they thought could get funded. Often, they were not even bringing their best ideas to the table."* (16) His suggestion to assess research proposals: it should be blinded with evaluators having no information on the applicant's background or publishing record. An approach that, as we shall see, FPE advocates as well.

Is there no way out of this dilemma? Will we have forever to be subjected to a hierarchical top-down approval to express ourselves?

From the perspective of college students and pupils in schools, this problem may not be so evident and it isn't debated in public journals. However, it is equally present and detrimental. Children are rarely allowed to observe, scrutinize, pore over and get deeper into a subject that attracts their attention and curiosity when doing so would disrupt the timeline of the preconceived curriculum which establishes what they must learn and in which what temporal order. They must obey a strict calendar in which everything is already decided in advance according to a detailed 'roadmap'. That innate curiosity and instinct to know which leads pupils into a 'dream state' is ignorantly suppressed and condemned as 'laziness' and 'passivity'. Instead, we should allow children to have their 'soul time' instead of forcefully pulling them from their contemplative state. This is one of the many ignorant behaviors of adults that impairs the child's ability to develop intuition, vision and creative skills, continuously breaking their concentration through a 45- or 60-minute rule and creating other adults who no longer have dreams or visions but then, paradoxically, complain about a youth who didn't learn to think critically and creatively.

As to funding mechanisms, they usually require an endless grant-writing at the expense of doing actual research. Conservative, closed-ended proposals have much better chances of success than innovative, open-ended proposals. Curiously, this has gone so far that there is even no longer a human individual, a 'dictator', or a 'big brother' responsible for this state of affairs. It is a system, a huge impersonal 'Matrix' which forces everyone, from the first-year student to the managing director of big institutions, to align themselves to it.

Those who have had some life experience inside the academy and have a minimum of sincerity, especially with themselves, know all too well how the myth that universities are about the education of students is something perpetrated only to get funding and public support. Universities are a managerial system almost entirely focused on providing faculties with the money and workforce they want. Teaching is perceived by most professors, especially those leading research groups, as a burden to be minimized as much as possible – a burden that has no place in the minds of those ruling the academic machinery. Almost all human and financial resources are put into the maintenance of the status quo in the face of any potential effort that could lead to a change.

The lack of promotion of independent thought and original, individual, spontaneous, creative learning, thinking, and research has its roots also in a false sense of fairness and equality, according to which everyone must do the same things and learn the same things, and which unconsciously perceives people with unusual skills and a strong sense for independent work as a menace to the system, contrary to what is usually declared officially. 'Teamwork' and 'excellence' are the mantras. But while acquiring social skills which make us fit for teamwork is something that should be encouraged, we should not forget that real excellence comes from within. Teamwork is fine, it is not only desirable but also necessary. But if teamwork is pushed too far, when the individual is completely sacrificed at the altar of the collective, then it becomes a form of stagnation and conformity that kills one's own possibilities of self-expression and evolution. The creative thinker, following research programmes which are presently in fashion, established by senior scientists, and obeying their orders, in some sense, might also learn something. Teamwork would provide an illuminating experience, in fact, but only when it is an exception, not the rule as it is actually. While the common belief is that the controversy pro and vs. teamwork is new, I found it somewhat amusing to discover how in an old documentary, an American mathematician, Prof.

R.L. Moore, inventor of the Inquiry Based Learning (IBL) method, already in 1966 stated: *"There's so much talk nowadays about teamwork, in favour of it, but that doesn't mean that everybody feels that way at all."* (17) After more than half a century the very same talk continues and nothing has changed. We will raise this issue again later in the book by comparing it with another possible option which compromises between individual work and teamwork: spontaneous cooperation.

Something similar on these lines can be said about competition and extroversion. Competition plays a healthy role as long it is meant to find the best solution or product. It becomes detrimental when it takes the form of a system that humiliates some to the advantage of others only because of their personality. An example is how our institutions are designed to favour extrovert students and best talkers promoting them later to leading positions, while introverts and contemplatives are penalized because of their intrinsic character that finds it hard to compete in the field of PR. There is no evidence that the former perform better than the latter, and it is time to recognize that solitude can be as much a key to innovation as teamwork is. Moreover, there is no scientific evidence to support our deeply engraved conviction that competition is the best stimulus for productivity. There is, in fact, plenty of evidence from psychology and brain research that cooperation is much more effective than competition. If our blind faith in competition would open itself to a cooperative alternative, that alone could transform the world.

I would like to ask: is it better to study for a degree at Stanford or follow a course in calligraphy instruction at some unknown college? Steve Jobs couldn't see the 'value in attending a college and at that time had no idea what to do with his life', until he decided to look for what was for him 'far more interesting following [his] curiosity and intuition for something beautiful in a way science can't capture, and fascinating', i.e. calligraphy. (18) Just this furnished him with the skills to apply and integrate the typesetting in computers we all know nowadays. Where did his passion come from? Where did his vision of 'connecting the dots' come from? From the mind or the soul? And what if he had followed the advice of the 'learning professional'? What about Steve Wozniak, the inventor and co-founder with Jobs of the Apple personal computer company in 1976 that revolutionized the world of IT? He developed the Apple prototypes at home, not at Hewelett Packard, from which he resigned, or at the University of California, Berkeley, from which he withdrew. A similar story can be told about the Microsoft Corporation founder, Bill Gates. According to his biography (19), he did not have a definite study plan while a student at university, and he finally dropped out of Harvard to start the computer software company. What did huge and rich industries like HP or IBM, or prestigious academic institutions like UC Berkeley or Harvard miss or lack in order to achieve what a few young men did?

The death of creativity in an era of big science

The lack of creativity is not only inherent in a standard industrial approach but reflects itself also in larger research projects. It impacts modern schools and academia in their way of thinking, conceiving, and doing science. Its organizational conception has become commonplace in the large laboratories, those forming part of the worldwide big science initiatives. Big science is one of the most prominent and visible symbols of our age, and has been criticized for several reasons. However, the connection between the dark side of huge scientific projects and that of modern education is rarely highlighted.

The first big science project dates back to the times of WWII, and was the famous Manhattan Project. As is well known, this was a US-led research project, with some participation of other nations like the UK and Canada, that aimed at the construction of the first atom bomb, which was used later on Hiroshima and Nagasaki. Was it a success? In a certain sense it was, since it obtained the desired result and put an end to WWII. But it may not be a coincidence that one of the first big science projects came from the military, just the kind of environment which places at the centre the protection of the collective, against the interests and development of the individual. Anyway, the Manhattan Project came into existence in an atmosphere of war, fear, and distrust, leading to a huge loss of lives making it clear what a horror the nuclear holocaust could be. Nobody today takes this as an example to justify funds for projects.

Shortly after the Manhattan Project, the international community launched a large-scale research study aimed at obtaining a controlled nuclear-fusion reactor (the type of nuclear energy that makes stars burn) that was supposed to save us from future energy crises. But after more than half a century it remains unclear if it is possible even in principle to build one (nobody knows how to build the chamber that must efficiently contain the hot plasma without a risk of meltdown).

In the 1960s we had the Apollo Project, and about 10 years later astronauts were sent to the moon. But today, almost half a century later, everyone realizes that it was only about the cold war and politics, certainly not about science and the wellbeing of humanity as a whole. And, frankly, where is the 'giant leap for mankind'?

How many remember that, more or less about the same time, former US President Richard Nixon announced to the world that the 'war on cancer' began, financing with billions of dollars research against the 'disease of the century'? Again, after half a century, despite some progress, cancer remains the lethal disease of the new century too. While the death rate is declining steadily, after all these enormous investments in cancer research and therapy, the net result is very disappointing when compared to initial expectations. It is still a matter of dispute as to whether this lower mortality rate is due to the effectiveness of therapies (which are frequently plagued by heavy collateral effects, sometimes deadly themselves) or whether it must be credited to other factors, such as the decline in smoking, the use of early detection tests and the utilization of frequent screenings.

And what about the space shuttle project? It was supposed to become a cheap and reusable space transportation system. Instead, it has turned out to be a bottomless pit. And despite the clear evidence coming from previous historical experience that robotic space exploration produced much better results of scientific interest, and for much less money, than sending humans in space, the international community nevertheless pursued the launch of the International Space Station (ISS). It is an impressive piece of space-engineering achievement, as a great YouTube video channel where millions can contemplate the Earth from space. Perhaps this turned to be its greatest gift to humanity, indeed. But we should remember that it was advertised for its potential, such as for the production of new medicines and material science, but so far not much has come out of it.

In March 2000, former President Bill Clinton made a similar announcement, this time about the mapping of the human genome. Billions upon billions of dollars were invested in order to open humanity to the 'genetic personalized medicine'. This was the promise. A dozen years later the widespread consensus is that the human genome project was quite disappointing. It turned out that 'life is complicated' (20), since our cells are much more complex than we suspect. Therefore, any hope of healing genetic diseases remains as far off as ever.

And it is now for at least three decades that we have been hearing about the coming age of a bio-engineering and agrarian revolution that would save us from genetic diseases and feed a world plagued by overpopulation. But, while we are still waiting for some sort of 'personalized medicine', people in the so-called third world countries continue to starve. Genetic engineering and the application of genetically modified organisms in the food industry remain a controversial topic more than ever, and, among fears, ethical concerns, and lack of real progress, continue to raise scepticism. After the first cloning in 1998 of the sheep Dolly, the world was thrilled by the prospects of big-science medicine, in particular by the growth of stem cells with the promise to grow human organs as transplants. What happened to the radical breakthroughs? Much was promised, but as of 2019 not much was delivered. As biomedical engineer Professor Michael Sefton put it, they had been 'hopelessly naive', since 'organs are immensely complex' (21).

Recently, stem cell research has been overshadowed by the advent of yet another big-science project: CRISPR (clustered regularly interspaced short palindromic repeats), a genome-editing technique that allows researchers to alter DNA sequences and modify gene function. CRISPR has inspired hope about its potential applications, from gene therapy to the improvement of crops. However, its promise also raises ethical concerns. It caused a worldwide outcry when it became known that a Chinese researcher claimed to have produced the world's first gene-edited babies. (22) This, when it was already known that gene editing produces unwanted DNA deletions (23) and it is clear that this technology won't fully fix sick people anytime soon. (24)

On top of that is a growing awareness of how bad science is determining not just some scientific outcome but the lives or deaths of millions. A nice example of that is the account of Richard Harris, an American biomedical scientist, in his book "Rigor Mortis" (25), which describes how American taxpayers spend about half of the $30 billion in annual funding for biomedical research on studies that can't be replicated due to poor experimental design, improper methods and sloppy statistics. Morris describes a dysfunctional biomedical system in which good scientific criteria and rigorous methods have been replaced, much too often, by procedures that once would have been regarded as inexcusable but that nowadays are increasingly becoming the norm. What once was called the 'scientific method' is becoming *"an illusion of progress by wrapping incremental advances in false promises"*, as expressed by Sabine Hosselfelder, a German theoretical physicist at the University of Frankfurt who is also quite renowned for her criticism of how modern particle physics is managed and pursued. (26) Big science initiatives are no longer about creating enlightenment but, rather, excitement. Most of the money goes into producing papers with exciting but ultimately empty headlines. This self-sustaining multimedia hype-cycle creates research-bubbles which, sooner or later, become unsustainable and destined to burst. Meanwhile, politics is all too happy to jump into this self-sustaining circus and talk about international competitiveness to keep the money flowing. Yet the hard facts on the ground are lacking. In most cases, for these big science projects, tangible progress is difficult to see and real breakthroughs are not coming. The irony is that most scientists are well aware of this but prefer to keep going on. After all, they make a living out of it, and it is hard to escape the instinct of self-preservation. Additionally, those who find themselves too annoyed by it simply quit, as the author himself made eloquently clear with his own autobiographical introduction. The ones who survive are those who adapt best and are more prone to accepting the state of affairs. Many also like to convince themselves that the research is so big and so complex, it is a quite natural thing that requires more time. To reach the goal, we need another two or three decades. After that time has passed, they will retire and a new generation of scientists will take the lead, repeating the same argument as a mantra to justify another three decades of the same research with the same methods and the same mindset.

However, all this is not only a consequence of humanity's selfishness or bad faith.

The universe is revealing to our research, and upon closer inspection, an ever-increasing complexity that quickly is escaping the grasp of the analytic mind. Even our personal life, which is manifestly influenced by the very same scientific and technological revolution, has become increasingly complex to such a degree that it is unlikely it will remain still controllable for a long time. At some point a mental civilization which drives itself towards an ever-increasing complexity is doomed to collapse, or a relapse.

And yet, the lesson has still not been learned. Now we hear about other projects similar to the human genome mapping. For instance, the EU is willing to pump more than a billion euros into the 'human brain project' (HBP), which involves hundreds of researchers, from 135 partner institutions in 26 countries. In the words of its official website, it proposes to integrate everything we know about the brain into computer models and using these models to simulate the actual working of the brain. Ultimately, it will attempt to simulate the complete human brain (27). The project aims to build a full computer model of a functioning brain to simulate drug treatments. On the other side of the ocean, the BRAIN Initiative (Brain Research through Advancing Innovative Neurotechnologies) was announced by former US President Barack Obama administration on April 2, 2013, with the goal of mapping the activity of every neuron in the human brain, and projected to cost more than $300 million per year for ten years.

It seems that nobody recalls how, in the 1980s, the Japanese government had launched a similar project named 'Fifth Generation Computer Systems project' aimed at building AI on massively parallel computer platforms, but it soon turned out that it could not meet expectations. Intelligence's nature and workings are much harder to decipher than previously thought. Will modern supercomputers be more successful? There are good reasons to doubt that, and several neuroscientists have, in an open message to the European Commission, already criticized the HBP as highly 'controversial and divisive without transparency', with a call to eventually 'redirect the HBP funding to smaller investigator-driven neuroscience grants'. (28)

However, most of the attention moving around the AI sector is focused on self-driving cars. A vision of a future in which driverless cars and futuristic robotic automotive transportation systems dominate our daily lives is presently the dream hypnotizing the public thanks to a large media campaign that celebrates the supposedly great breakthroughs – and that, of course, the present industrial scene takes advantage of. Billions of dollars in R&D are spent and the world's largest corporations, such as Google and Apple, are betting everything on this emerging technology. Again, thousands are employed as raw working labor to realize this goal in a concerted effort inside a huge industrial and managerial think tank environment. One wonders: Will it be worthwhile? The answer obviously depends on the success or failure of this line of research. If it will be successful, fine. However, the initial enthusiasm is now fading because we are slowly but steadily realizing that driving a car is not at all that kind of mechanical task a machine can perform. Rather, it requires knowledge and the ability to predict human behavior, which, obviously, only humans possess. When several accidents occurred, some with causalities, and received a significant amount of media attention, things became even worse. It is now clear that fully automated driverless cars are not to be expected soon.

If children, in their families and/or schools, were allowed to learn to look inside themselves instead of always being forced to externalize their consciousness, becoming aware of how their thoughts and feelings manifest and of how their own brains work, as adults they would have no issue with realizing that the cognitive functions at work while one drives a car have nothing to do with the kind of functions AI processes mimic (deep learning neural networks, etc.) and are supposed to lead us to build autonomous vehicles. It is not a matter of analytic thinking and scientific knowledge; it is a matter of knowing themselves. This is something most of us have never learned (or were taught to forget and ignore) – a fact especially true among scientists who were trained with empiric externalizing thinking.

The next big things that run in parallel with self-driving cars nowadays are the so-called 'quantum computers'. As the name indicates, quantum computers take advantage of quantum physical processes that, in principle, would allow them to solve certain kinds of problems that ordinary computers can't tackle or can tackle only with much longer processing times. The idea is not new; it dates back to Richard Feynman, the famous American physicist and Nobel laureate, who in 1982 showed how conventional computers could, in principle, be outperformed by a hypothetical universal quantum simulator. However, only in recent times has the technology become mature enough to encourage scientists and investors to consider its practical realization. The hype surrounding quantum computing spread fast when, around the mid-end of the 1990s, theoretical progress was made and IBM began working on it. It also spread about ten years later, when Google jumped into the race. This is, again, another technology that was – and still is – supposed to change the world and all our lives but that, so far, has not. After over two decades of intense R&D and significant funding, the results are disappointingly far from the originally predicted ones. Google announced that it would reach 'quantum supremacy' – that is, the realization of a 49-qubit (quantum-bit) quantum computer device capable of solving at least one problem that a classical computer cannot – by the end of 2017. In fact, in March 2018 the company realized a 56-qubit quantum computer which, however, could not perform any computation more efficiently than conventional IT could. Quantum bits are plagued by noise which cannot be easily eliminated. Now scientists speak of thousands, if not millions, of qubits necessary to build such a machine, which means it will not become a reality anytime soon. The more time passes by, the more it becomes clear that the technical challenges to overcome are much more complex than previously expected. Moreover, there is growing skepticism over whether quantum computing will be able in practice, or even in principle, to outperform classical computation devices. It remains to be seen whether quantum computers will ever live up to the hype. What is certain is that the speed of development and the pace of the technological advance of quantum computers is far slower than that which produced the good-old PCs we work with nowadays. The fact is, again, the expectations which were so excitingly announced years, if not decades, earlier were not met and the number of skeptics who express doubts regarding the practical realizability of quantum computers is growing. (29)

Admittedly, there were also some successful big-science projects. The most notorious one that comes to mind might be the Hubble Space Telescope or the Cassini interplanetary probe to Saturn (but these underlined again the success of unmanned space exploration vs. human space exploration) or that which led to the discovery of gravitational waves that were predicted by Einstein's theory of general relativity. Another example is CERN, the European Organization for Nuclear Research, which, with its particle accelerators in Geneva, contributed to confirming the standard model of particle physics. But its particle accelerators did not after all lead to a big conceptual change in the theories, they merely confirmed the theoretical predictions that particle physicists had already made. And, apart from a small elite group that can occupy themselves with foundational issues, CERN is mainly a huge industrial-engineering enterprise, where only seldom do novel ideas come into being. Curiously, John Bell, an Irish particle physicist at CERN in the 1960s, mainly concerned with accelerator design, paradoxically made his greatest contribution instead in the foundations of quantum physics. However, he worked on that pursuit during his free time, on weekends.

CERN's last creation, the world's biggest particle accelerator, the Large Hadron Collider (LHC), has still to prove itself. So far (as of 2019) it has only discovered something predicted by theory, the Higgs boson. The LHC seems unable to achieve what it was designed for: to find the signature for any new physics, like some hint that could lead us beyond the standard model of particle physics, or a paradigm shift like Einstein's relativity or quantum mechanics did. Superstrings and supersymmetry are very complex theories which were developed in a concerted effort of most theoretical physics departments all over the world to go beyond this standard model. An exaggerated amount of resources and young minds were devoted for this goal to the detriment of other lines of research and promising developments in physics. This should have led us beyond our present understanding of the world, but experimental evidence seems to cast doubts on that happening, and no new 'quantum revolution' is in sight. It seems that Nature didn't appreciate the human effort to decipher its complexity, and decided that things should work otherwise. The lack of evidence for supersymmetry or anything beyond the standard model of particles is leading to a crisis in physics. (30) (31) A 'nightmare scenario', as some physicists call it, is rising on the horizon. The nightmare is that probably thousands of physicists have spent the last 30 years running after a chimera.

Anyway, apart from some specific successful cases, history suggests that the excessive focus on the big-science approach we could observe in more than half a century must make way for a more critical view. We can now confidently say that—despite the strong popular media coverage whose hypes always tend to suggest otherwise—in retrospective, facts show how the success and turnout of these huge scientific efforts can be considered as quite limited compared to their original expectations. People, especially those who have to pay taxes in times of financial crises, are getting more and more skeptical and nervous towards titanic investments into gigantic science projects. And rightly so. It must be said that those responsible for this state of affairs were to a large extent not only politicians, but also great men of science (one case that comes to my mind was the American astronomer and TV commentator Carl Sagan, lobbying for sending men to Mars), and who were, and continue to be, ready to sacrifice several smaller good science projects in the name of big science. And interestingly, the most valuable results emerging from these mammoth projects were to be found in the field of pure science, not in the applied sciences. Which again underlines how unreasonable it is to ask a priori for practical results. Maybe it is time to learn that it is Nature that should guide us to potential applications, instead of us trying to predict it with our limited understanding.

So, should we therefore stop spending money on science projects? No, quite the contrary: we should double our spending for science. And, of course, there are things that will never be achieved without international big-science initiatives. Building a space station, sending humans to the moon and Mars, or building nuclear fusion reactors will still require a joint effort on the part of thousands of specialists working hard in a concerted manner for years, if not decades.

However, we should focus the resources on the right projects, and especially in the right manner. And who decides what the right ones are supposed to be? Of course, this will forever remain a subjective point of view. But what about funding several small science projects instead of a single big-science one? Does it really make sense to divert all the funds, efforts, and skills of people into the n-th mammoth project? What about spending several smaller amounts of money in many risky projects than huge amounts into mainstream ones? Albert Fert and Peter Grünberg were awarded the Nobel Prize in physics in 2007 for the discovery of Giant Magnetoresistance which allowed the manufacture of modern hard drive GB storing technologies. They developed their technique investing about €5000. Three years later, Andre Geim and Kostya Novoselov received the Nobel Prize for their experiments on the two-dimensional material, graphene. They had extracted single-atom-thick layers from bulk graphite lifting them off with a simple adhesive tape.

Still, paradoxically, it is easier to get mi-bi-trillions in funds for conventionally accepted lines of research than a few thousand dollars for small and cheap original projects. It is sometimes almost impossible to obtain as modest a grant as \$50,000 for a postdoc, working on a little but novel and original non-traditional line of research, just because it is new (i.e. risky), original (i.e. of uncertain outcome), and non-mainstream (read: it is about giving out money to a 'black sheep' who does not bleat with the flock). Statistical and historic records show (32) that the scientific impact per dollar is turning out to be progressively lower for large grant-holders, and that the hypothesis that large grants lead to great discoveries is inconsistent. We should reconsider the current wave of enthusiasm for stratospheric projects. This is not about entirely abolishing big science, which might still be indispensable in some fields, but it is about rediscovering the potential of the small enterprises and initiatives, but especially that of the individual scientist.

The real point is that despite all these huge investments in science, academic projects, and consistent cultural and scientific promotions, there has been no real paradigm shift. Sure, you will be able to name a lot of great scientists, Nobel laureates, and geniuses who have made groundbreaking discoveries up until our times. But where are the new Copernicuses, Keplers, Galileos, Newtons, or Einsteins? It seems that after Einstein the scientific genius has become extinct. (33) It was not big science or huge industrialized and highly organized academic structures that convinced a doctor of canon law, like Nicolaus Copernicus, that the Sun is at the centre of the solar system. Heliocentrism was a principle embraced for some very simple observational and personal aesthetic reasons. Big science did not lead to new great paradigm shifts like that of relativity, which was sparked by 'Mister Nobody', Albert Einstein, working in a Swiss patent office. No new 'quantum revolution' is in sight like that introduced around the beginning of the 20th century by some professor with zero research funds like Max Planck, but who informed the world that he had a crazy idea he himself could hardly believe in: energy must be absorbed and emitted in discrete quantities, not in a continuous fashion. Nowadays we are looking for the theory which should unify gravity with electromagnetic and nuclear forces. Physicists have been searching for it for the last 70 years, but still there is today no new Planck alleviating their pains. Are the great paradigm shifts, the Copernican revolutions of the past, definitely over? Why don't we see also today new groundbreaking theories, like that of relativity and quantum mechanics which changed our worldview, considering the great efforts and expenditures of big science? Of course, lots of original ideas are seen today too, but most come from complicated calculations, not from some fundamentally new 'way of seeing' the world. New first principles are lacking. Why? How could that be? Shouldn't a world where science is so central, so much encouraged, and so well-funded, reserve ample space for creative scientific thinkers?

Ernest Rutherford, the physicist and Nobel laureate who is considered the father of modern nuclear physics, is often cited as being the initiator of modern big science. He led the Cavendish Laboratory in Cambridge, UK, from 1919 until his death in 1937. Under his direction other researchers and students also made historic discoveries in atomic physics, and many of them received the Nobel prize too. Yet much of the work in his laboratory used simple, inexpensive devices, and things did not proceed as one would expect in a top research centre. A former student of his (and also a Nobel laureate), James Chadwick confessed: *"I did a lot of experiments about which I never said anything. Some of them were quite stupid. I suppose I got that habit or impulse, or whatever you'd like to call it, from Rutherford. He would do some damn silly experiments at times, and we did some together. They were really damned silly. But if we'd gotten a positive result, they wouldn't have been silly."* (34) While Mark Oliphant, another student and co-worker of Rutherford, said: 'Rutherford also lectured on the atom, with great enthusiasm, but not always coherently or well prepared.' (35)

How is it that a laboratory with simple equipment and roughly thirty research students who (more or less secretly) made 'stupid' and 'silly' experiments, and were lectured by an 'unprepared' person, could nevertheless produce an impressive number of Nobel laureates, and rewrite entire chapters of 20th century physics, while so many other big-science projects, funded with billions of dollars and run by thousands of scientists, failed to furnish nearly comparable results? There is a wide range of evidence showing that research effort is rising substantially while research productivity is declining sharply. (36)

The typical objection is that some discoveries will never again come from little projects, and the times of the lonely genius working in the patent office, or the science project led by a bunch of smart but unorganized people, are over. The testing of new theories, and the advancement of science, now need a huge, concentrated financial and human effort that little research laboratories can't afford. Nowadays, interdisciplinary collaborations of big teams with complex, hi-tech hardware are necessary if we want to discover the secrets of the universe. This is the argument. And, admittedly, there is some truth in that. Without the Hubble Space Telescope and the large colliders, our understanding of the universe would not have progressed in some sectors of fundamental science. But a verdict that the times of the intuitive, independent, and original thinkers (and, yes, also those of the banned 'lonely thinker') are over has no grounds. They must inevitably come back, since creativity and curiosity are intrinsic to human nature, and form part of an inner expression of the Homo sapiens sapiens, and are not something that comes and goes.

Behind these gigantic technological efforts stand, first and foremost, commercial interests. However, there also stand unjustified, and to some extent irrational, beliefs and hopes, sometimes strongly promoted by quite smart intellectuals. Such beliefs include the notion that these technologies will project us towards a future society in which everything is completely automated and regulated by some futuristic AI and computer technology that will do all the work for us. The most optimistic scenario foresees humanoid robots which will take up all our jobs and our physical and intellectual activities, allowing the human species to lean back and enjoy a life-long vacation. This wishful thinking is, however, contradicted by the last two centuries of technological evolution. The trend towards replacing human labor with automatized machinery killed jobs; it also created new necessities and consumer desires which quickly demanded new skills and competencies that were formerly unknown or unnecessary. These illusions are not new. Already in 1930, the British economist John Maynard Keynes predicted that, due to extensive industrialization and economic and technological progress, by the time his grandchildren had grown up, we would be working only 15 hours a week. (37) This was not only a much too optimistic projection, as a 40-hour week remains a normal state of affairs, but, almost a century later, the contrary tendency is quite evident. A workweek that is 50 or 60 hours in length is no longer something which burdens only managers or slaves. People who experience so much stress that they develop burnout syndrome aren't rarities, either. The bottom line is that the progress of science or big-science, technology and the economy alone won't lead us to a better and more relaxed society if we do not also grow something inside us which progresses in parallel with the outward conditions.

The point is that we are living in times where the creative thinker, guided by an inner intrinsic motivation, is simply de-selected by the system a priori. The problem is that science has become too 'central', in the sense that it is too centralized, industrialized. Big science has become also a big enterprise with a big army, organized according to a managerial top-down hierarchy of subordinate and obedient employees who are pressured continuously by deadlines assigned from the top, which tells them what to do, how to do it, and when to do it. A system that officially tells us to encourage independent thinking, while the truth goes in the exactly opposite direction. In its intrinsic structure and organization, it is incapable of leaving much space, if any, for the personal and spontaneous development of the genius. It should have been clear since the beginning that it couldn't deliver the promises it made. It is time to rethink all that from the ground up.

The pedagogical 'black hole' of high schools

In this historical, social, and economic context of industrialization, those who have suffered the most in terms of intellectual growth and renewal are high schools and universities. The attention devoted to the pedagogical aspects of higher education and that devoted to primary education are orders of magnitudes apart. There is a hiatus, a 'black hole' that divides the two worlds in pedagogical science. It is particularly in the domain of secondary school and college levels upwards that we urgently need new methodological approaches to studying and learning.

The roots of this cultural crisis, stemming from a centuries-long stagnation, can be found in the psychological mechanism that dominates our daily life, apart from the historical development of education, industry, economy, and science. One of these is what I would call the 'learning-slave effect'. There are slaves who know that they are slaves, but there are also slaves who don't really realize that they are slaves. We live in a cultural context that has convinced and manipulated us to such a degree that the system we live in must be considered the best one possible. Especially when it comes to higher education, where we must learn professional skills and absorb huge amounts of data and stuff, we tend to convince ourselves that there could be no better way to achieve some skills and objectives than to adhere to and accept the present paradigm, as if it were given by a supernatural law. A frequent statement coming from young students annoyed by their school system is that their anguish is a 'necessary evil', an 'unavoidable suffering', as if it were imposed not by a human made organization, but by a law of nature, a mathematical necessity of life that can't be changed, not even in principle.

In fact, conventional schools, especially high schools, are the only institutionalized forms of submission which are still accepted without any critical thinking, even in the most democratic countries. Young students are rarely allowed to learn what really interests them, but must usually learn a lot of stuff that nobody knows what it is really useful for. With strictly defined curricula, they are told what to learn, how to learn it, and in what time frame they have to learn. Not much room is left for the realization of one's own ideas and interests through a self-chosen path of study. But lots of uninteresting useless mind stuff has to be absorbed according to a 'sponge principle'. All is pushed forward by external pressures, and almost never by intrinsic motivation. Everything is standardized, and everyone must learn the same things and do so in the same manner. The teacher is the authority students are not allowed to choose, and whom they must obey. Teachers are not asked to be a mentor, a friend, or a helper, but must pursue a school teaching which is about crowd control and babysitting. They are in a power position which is usually exerted through the sword of Damocles of grades. Except corporal punishment, which fortunately has been banned in several countries (though not in all), many other sorts of punishing measures are still permitted. Schools demand obedience and responsibility, but paradoxically do not allow for self-discipline and self-responsibility. There is no democratic participation of students in the school's staff meetings, decisions at which cannot be appealed. Students are forced to sit at the classroom desk for several hours a day, while modern research has repeatedly and clearly shown how detrimental this is for their cognition process. Things must be learned with a repeated 45-60-minute rhythm, when it is well known from psychology that our attention quickly drops to its minimum level after 20-30 minutes. Compulsory medieval rituals are still in place, like pupils standing up with a welcoming chant when the teacher enters the classroom, or the ringing of the end-of-class bell, which is awaited by many anxiously. We are told that young people should learn to think critically, to be independent, and take their future into their hands, while school teaches them exactly the contrary down to the most minute and ridiculous detail. It is the only place left in our society where even going to the bathroom needs permission. Children have no choice other than to obey the grownups, who are themselves only the 'longa manus' of the state. Conflict resolution, tolerance, respect, the art of compromise, and empathy are taught in a dry theoretical way, but are not learned as an organized, participatory, and a lived, experiential process. A marvellous example of this that I could observe as a teacher is how nowadays it is quite in fashion to organize classes of nonviolent communication which are held by just those teachers with the harshest and most rigid character and who aren't themselves able to put in practice what they teach. Schools were and still are a stronghold of authoritarianism which remains untouched, unmovable, granitic.

The irony of all this is that even those teachers who would like to change something in this intricate and suffocating system are themselves compelled to follow the strict rules imposed by an abstract power system where nobody is personally in charge as a human being. Several good teachers have tried to make a difference, but could not go beyond a limit imposed by a tightly conservative educational system. The importance of teachers has been shown to be decisive, but the problem goes much beyond the quality of teachers. It is useless, and also unfair, to consider teachers as solely responsible for an educational structure the future of which is already visible. When society begins to awaken and realize this state of affairs, schools as we know them presently are doomed to crumble under their own weight. With or without good teachers.

My dream would be to create a free-progress secondary high school (FPH), which could also serve as a basis for a free-progress university (FPU) later, where students can learn, study, and prepare themselves in complete freedom for future jobs without the pressure of examinations and the straitjacket of curricula. But we are so accustomed to the present system, which has gone into each of our fibers and every cell of our brain, that we consider it normal, an inevitable malady we have to take onto ourselves to be successful in life and find a job. This conviction is still deeply engraved in most of the young people who attend the schools and universities oriented along this mindset and educational paradigm. Schools produce 'learning-slaves', and after all also 'teaching-slaves', who differ from industrial slaves only by the fact that they don't know it.

But signs of change are visible on the horizon. For example, in Germany, there is already a sort of experiment going on which tries to question the status quo. In 2007, a group of students from the city of Freiburg founded the 'Methodos' group. They moved away from the established school system to prepare themselves for the final secondary-education exam (Abitur), which allows college entrance. (38) (39) After several disappointing attempts to change the rules and didactical approaches from inside of their former schools (by the way, a Waldorf school), the group courageously took the decisive step, and left. They were looking for a school that fosters self-determined learning, personal development, competences, skills, learning by doing, social processes of teamwork, active participation, and time and space in which to reflect about their own interests, and about how to pursue them. Since there is no high school in Germany which allows for something alike, they decided to build their own school. They found a place where they could study together in groups, by an auto-didactical approach, and hired teachers who prepared them for the examinations. These, however, are chosen by the students themselves. Moreover, at 'Methodos', the teachers play the role of mentors who should counsel and help them, but are not hired as authorities imposed by an institution which they have to obey. According to the Methodos principle, only half of the time is devoted to preparation for the final exams. The other half of the time is devoted to learning in an organized team, and connected to their own interests, which may or may not form part of the official curricula.

However, while the case of Methodos is certainly an interesting precedent, it has also severe limitations. It is not really a high school, but a study group which meets in more or less derelict rooms, and has less than one year in time to prepare itself for the final secondary school examinations. With the end of the year nearing, it becomes increasingly difficult not to feel the pressure of the imminent exams.

What we are lacking, therefore, is a real FPH, which students can attend throughout the last four or five years of their higher education, and not by leaving the conventional school at the last year. This would allow students to learn much more freely, and with less time pressure, more or less like what is being done in the so-called democratic or Sudbury schools (that will be discussed in a forthcoming section). A 'democratic high school' could be conceived as one where students should not be forced to pursue an external certificate, where they could learn and live freely working instead towards the creation of a learning portfolio (according to rules we will describe in the next sections), eventually complemented with a written research thesis. Those students who wish to receive a certificate that allows entrance to conventional colleges could take a different track à la Methodos. But, even in that case, the four- or five-year-long high school journey will permit them to experience a completely different learning environment than that of conventional high schools. For example, only during the last year of their particular course would they have to undergo the examination process, but during the first three or four years they could express their intellectual interests freely, and choose independently the learning methods that best suit them.

I don't believe that the pedagogical principles, the learning modalities, or the internal or bureaucratic structure of an FPS and FPH would differ very much from those of an FPU. There can, of course, arise differences in some respects and details. However, the foundations, at least in their psychological principles based on freedom and self-expression, are not likely to differ much. Therefore, the analysis that follows will not differentiate much between these cases. The principles of a new education that are outlined in the following sections should be as valid for a new free-progress school, high school as for colleges and universities.

Past and present attempts to reform education

One frequently hears people talking about the need for education to be thought through afresh and reformed with new ideas or novel approaches.

However, many ideas have already been worked out and we don't need to invent the wheel from scratch again. In the last two-and-a-half centuries, there has been no lack of alternative ideas – only a lack of courage to put these into practice. What we are trying to do here is not so much to propose a particularly novel educational philosophy but, rather, a synthesis of some of these approaches and ideas adapted to a modern context and eventually re-elaborated from a different perspective.

Already in 1762, the French philosopher Jean-Jacques Rousseau, who influenced the European Enlightenment, wrote 'Emile', a treatise on education. (40) While an FPE paradigm would reject some of his ideas (such as the necessity of strictly differentiating between male and female education reflecting the submissive role of women), several others are surprisingly real. Rousseau warned against imposing onto pupils too early a bookish knowledge which should not replace the knowledge that the sensory experience of the world and manual skills could deliver. Feelings and emotions shouldn't be cast out in favour of the reasoning mind, as the latter can be perfected only by the former. This idea seemed to be too romantic and naive but, instead, has been repeatedly confirmed by modern brain research. (41) (42)

Interestingly, the application of pedagogic thinking that is supposed to foster the individual creative spirit has been largely debated in the frame of pre-college/university environment since the 17th century. Between 1780 and 1800, the Swiss pedagogue and educational reformer Johann Heinrich Pestalozzi conceived of educational methods based on individual differences and vocational self-determination. In 1810, Wilhelm von Humboldt, a Prussian philosopher and government functionary, tried, in vain, to reform the German school system according to a scheme where education is not only meant for making a living, but also emphasizes the skills of learning to learn. In 1897, the American philosopher and psychologist John Dewey published his pedagogic creed of 'progressive education'. Progressive education emphasizes among other things personalized education, lifelong learning by direct experience, doing rather than text-book reading, group work, cooperative learning, project-based learning, and school as community life. Dewey held that 'all education proceeds by the participation of the individual in the social consciousness of the race'. (43). Dewey's ideal of 'progress', however, can be considered only a small subset of the concept of free-progress education we are trying to develop here. About 1907, Maria Montessori, the first woman in Italy to earn a doctorate, founded several schools based on a new pedagogy which bears her name. The Montessori method is now known worldwide for its education of children which emphasizes independence, freedom, and respect for a child's natural psychological development. About the same time, in Austria, Rudolf Steiner's pedagogy with his anthroposophical view of the human being and its associated movement, founded the Waldorf schools and which I have already described in some detail at the beginning of this book. Later, in the years following WWII, the Reggio Emilia approach, founded by Loris Malaguzzi in the Italian city of Bologna, realized that, if children are given opportunities to express themselves, and are free to explore, they become able to self-guide their own development. Perhaps the most interesting and relevant case, which might prove to be an inspiration for an FPH and an FPU, are democratic schools. The Summerhill School in 1921 and Sudbury-Valley-Schools in the 1960th will be described in more detail further on.

These were only some of the several other alternative schools that came into being in the last century. At the same time, alternative approaches have been strenuously resisted in the case of higher education. The novel, liberating methodology that these pedagogies introduced in the early stages of the educational process has been stubbornly denied access in its later stages. There is apparently this persistent assumption that only children deserve the freedom to express their creativity and imagination while learning. Even among the most advanced and open-minded pedagogies, there is this granitic conviction that once a young student enrols in university, the ideal of free learning must be set aside. Few appear to question the belief that, after a specific point in age, learning can't be done otherwise than by resorting to the good old system made up of sterile notions of learning, exams, grades, and certificates. The author does not know of any proposal, apart from a notable single exception (9), to reform post-secondary school learning according to precepts and ideals based on freedom, creativity, and personal development in research and intellectual inquiry. It seems that didactics and pedagogy are considered disciplines which have to deal only with little children, perhaps some retarded teenager, but not with adults. This is one of the most deep-rooted convictions of our society, psychology being no exception, that is producing a constantly increasing tension between the potentialities of adult individuals and their effective freedom to express them. It would not be surprising to see that this tension might reach a breaking point erupting in new forms of dissatisfaction, revolts, and possibly even violence, among those apparently most skilled, and later others without their being able to explain the deeper motives for their actions.

There has, however, been a more recent burst of interest in education. One has only to carry out some simple research on the web to see how many are praising freedom, creativity, and intuition, which have seemingly become rare stuff in our established institutions. In Germany, the Methodos group (already mentioned) was born, and it could be considered the transition link between high school and university. The debate on education is raging, and hopefully it will add some sparkle to the argument. One of the most notable names as international advisor on education is the already cited Sir Ken Robinson. For a broad spectrum of the ideas and initiatives emerging around the issue of education, it would be worthwhile to look up websites such as TED (44). Here we hear people speaking about great ideas and wonderful initiatives. For example, David Helfand outlines Quest University Canada's programme that aims at educating students for an interdisciplinary lifetime of learning, with intensive short 'blocks' courses. (45) It is indeed an interesting attempt that tries to break through the status quo of the established academic habits. Elizabeth Gilbert wonders about the elusive creative genius (46). Charles Leadbeater discovers how learning begins by formulating questions instead of imparting knowledge, how the collaborative process leads to innovation even in slums (47), and how the future will be that of mass participation and creativity. Susan Cain looks at the power of introversion, challenging the common trend of groupthink. 'Stop the madness for constant group work', she says. (48) (49)

Meanwhile, neuroscience builds bridges with education, and neurobiology is now discovering the connections between brain functions and the development of creativity. (50) (51) The Association for Contemplative Mind in Higher Education (52) connects a network of leading institutions and academics committed to the recovery and development of the contemplative dimension of teaching, learning, and knowing in higher education. It looks for contemplative practices such as mindfulness that specifically apply to higher education settings and pedagogical developments.

The Internet also offers Massive Open Online Courses (MOOC) for academic education programmes. Blended learning has been conceived as an education programme in which students learn at home through online content as well as at a supervised brick-and-mortar location away from home. (53) 'Flip teaching', based on peer instruction, an interactive teaching method developed by Harvard Professor Eric Mazur in the early 1990s, is a form of blended learning in which students learn by watching video lectures at home, and later discuss it and do 'homework' in class with the teacher offering personalized guidance instead of lecturing. The Khan Academy has a non-profit educational website that has as its stated mission to provide 'a free world-class education for anyone anywhere' and offers free online courses from algebra to computer science, from world history to finance. (54) Sugata Mitra, Professor of Educational Technology at Newcastle University in the UK, conducted his now-famous 'hole-in-the-wall' experiment, in which children in Indian slums were given access to computers with educational software, and were let completely free to learn whatever they wanted to without intervention from teachers. It turned out that they learned much faster than rich children with traditional schooling, and spontaneously taught themselves. The Self Organized Learning Environments (SOLE) initiative grew out of this experience. (55) Anya Kamenetz, author of the book DIY U (Do It Yourself University) (56) conceives of students helping one another acquire the knowledge they need on their own without being told how to act, or spending money in other traditional universities.

But, since all have some unique and individual skills and abilities in something, why can't everyone of us be a teacher in some area of competence? In fact, Jean-Pol Martin, a professor of foreign language teaching in Germany, introduced the 'learning by teaching' method (LdL. from the German 'Lernen durch Lehren'), a method whereby students themselves prepare and teach lessons to their classmates. (57) (58) Under the LdL method, students do not simply repeat the content that they learned previously by themselves, but also follow the didactical approach.

On the other side, MOOCs are still limited to professors and teachers with an academic title. Now why should we not conceive of a society where everyone is allowed to open a course in some subject, and teach others? The foreseeable future is that of a democratization not only of learning but equally that of teaching. A world where everyone who has usable knowledge, a good level of competence, and know-how, and does not need to be filtered out by a hierarchical, elitist, and closed-minded academic system, would become a place of an unprecedented and unpredictable cultural revolution. This is the kind of future that platforms like Udemy (59) are striving for.

There are other notable examples of attempts to reinvent schools and universities from scratch. The alternative educator and academician Mikhail Petrovich Shchetinin developed a model of a school and university for kids, the Lycee School at Tekos village near Gelendzhik in southern Russia, where ordinary pupils from more than 40 different nationalities, with little if any help from adult teachers, cover the whole 11-year curriculum of the Russian school system in just two years and get official bachelor's and master's degrees from accredited universities by the time they are seventeen. They design, build, decorate and administer their campus all by themselves without adult supervision. Children don't study in a classroom, they study subjects in groups and without teachers, the younger students learn from the older students and teach each other. (60) (61) On a similar track schools which adopt the natural learning method 'Laising', where founded in several countries. (62) (63) (64) (65) Lais or Laising is an old Indo-Germanic/Gothic word which means 'finding out', 'find and follow a track', related to German 'Gleis' which meant 'track' (in modern German it became the 'train platform'). Lais is a method which tries to remember natural, innate learning and living. Natural learning schools make use of the already innate learning skills in children. The acquisition of knowledge as a playful natural flow in the form of group experiences which awaken one's natural ability to learn with ease and joy.

Another interesting case in Germany which aims at establishing an alternative to the current higher education is the UniExperiment (66). According to some of its members it presents itself as a different option to university as *"a self-determined and self-organized community of people who learn and instruct themselves according to their interests. UniExperiment is an experiment where forms of self-determined learning can be realized and with space to question: themselves, others, rules, consciousness, perception, the world, institutions, science, intuition, etc. and leaving also room for people who (still) have no awareness for what could be "unbiased" questions. The students learn (also) from one another. The personal exchange about one's own perception should be as far as possible an extension of the subjective perception of the world, in the direction of greater objectivity. In the UniExperiment, there is no pre-defined formal hierarchy. Roles and functions of teachers and learners can change. If decisions are to be taken in the UniExperiment which concern several, these decisions are made by consensus."*

UniExperiment is so far still a somewhat vague and undefined attempt which has more questions than answers on how to bring to life a different university than the conventional hierarchical and grade based academy. It presently exists in a handful cities in Germany and materially consists of some rooms where people meet regularly and exchange their own views or occasionally hold seminars and lectures on specific topics, but is far from a full-fledged real university. It nevertheless deserves attention, especially for how it might develop in the future. Little things which go in the right direction can develop into great enterprises.

The Swaraj University in India has a two-year learning programme for youth focused on self-designed learning in the fields of ecological sustainability and social justice: 'Each person's learning program and curriculum is individualized according to his/her specific talents, questions and dreams.' They 'do not provide degrees,[but] rather encourage learners to develop their own portfolios and to develop their own livelihood projects and enterprise plans.' (67) The Kaospilot project, based in Denmark, is 'a hybrid business and design school, a multi-sided education in leadership and entrepreneurship' and provides 'space and a place where creatives and potential change-makers can develop the knowledge, skills, attitudes and competencies they need to fulfil their values and visions'. (68) Knowmads is a school in the Netherlands where 'young creative entrepreneurial spirits are educated to enable, facilitate, empower and inspire students to become change makers'. (69)

Most interesting is the Open Mater's Community (70) which goes in a similar direction we are thinking of here. It is a self-directed and self-organized community with an "in-person centred" path where the main idea is that no institution is needed to pursue a Master's Degree equivalent. Everyone can handcraft his/her own curriculum and both favour portfolio based studies. One can self-design a Master's on quite specific topics (such as in creative writing, storytelling, farming, etc.).

However, we would like to go even beyond that and conceive of full-fledged faculty divisions. Something which offers a real alternative for those who want to go through an established science or humanity faculty with a 3-5 yearlong curriculum or 'roadmap' (of course still self-designed), like what could be for instance the whole department of engineering, law, mathematics, philosophy, economics, etc. An alternative and a replacement to current faculties built upon a FPE paradigm. Otherwise, most present day students would not find FPE as a viable option.

An updated list of similar centres is available with the Alternative Education Resource Organization. (71)

Not only organisations but also worldwide known personalities are striving for a new concept of education. A notable example is Peter Gray, a research professor at Boston College, author of the bestselling book 'Free to Learn' (72) and whose research focuses on children's natural ways of learning and the life-long value of play. Gray is also the co-founder of the Alliance for Self-Directed Education. An education "*that derives from the self-chosen activities and life experiences of the person becoming educated, whether or not those activities were chosen deliberately for the purpose of education.*" (73) Based on this ideal, a community of 'Agile Learning Centers', an expanding network of micro-schools leveraging agile tools to support self-directed education, was founded throughout the US. (74)

One also finds – inspired by self-directed-learning principles – a small community of learners known as North Star (75), which offers an alternative to school. It is a place where teens learn at a pace and in the manner that suits them best. It is not a school; rather, through the assigning of a personal advisor, it helps teens prepare a customized academic plan based on their interests (making leaving school legal for youth under age 16 as a homeschooling proposal for submission to the local superintendent). North Star offers classes, workshops and tutorials that provide individual one-on-one meetings in subjects such as mathematics, foreign language, guitar and computer programming, as available. Most of its members are between the ages of 13 and 19; after that, they can choose to go on to college.

Perhaps the most well-known figure in the field is Sir Ken Robinson, an internationally recognized leader in the development of education who, as he sums on in his website (76)"works with governments, education systems, international agencies, global corporations and some of the world's leading cultural organizations to unlock the creative energy of people and organizations. He has led national and international projects on creative and cultural education in the UK, Europe, Asia and the United States. The embodiment of the prestigious TED Conference and its commitment to spreading new ideas, Sir Ken Robinson is the most watched speaker in TED's history. His 2006 talk, "Do Schools Kill Creativity" (77) has been viewed online over 40 million times and seen by an estimated 350 million people in 160 countries."

So, there is no lack of attempts to change something. The above-mentioned organisations, initiatives, and people who are devoting their energy to bring new forms of educational and pedagogical concepts into life and implementing them practically in schools or educational structures were just a few examples and probably represent only the tip of the iceberg. At a local level in every country, a lot of other similar projects and personalities struggle for a change. But have they caused a change?

Certainly not in my country. In my brief but intense three-year experience as a school teacher, I never heard even once of my colleagues mentioning anything of the above alternative education approaches. Hundreds of millions of people throughout the world browse these websites or click on K. Roberts' YouTube videos, but most school teachers do not even know of their existence. Almost no pedagogue working in schools and universities feels these worth mentioning, much less would they think of them as something that could be implemented as a model in the present system. Most of them are probably even not aware of its existence and, even if they are, seem not to be interested in it anyway. Schools remain what they have always been and there is no sign that they are going to reconsider what they are: impenetrable and immutable strongholds that isolate themselves from any attempt or proposal of change. These new educational groups or movements and the official educational structures with their teachers are like two parallel universes that refuse to make contact.

On the other hand, I have the feeling that most of these initiatives are limited to very specific fields, or allow only limited freedom (many are still based on the exam + grade system), or are still experimenting at an amateurish level, and have not progressed much beyond the dominant established paradigm. Some focus exclusively on primary- or secondary-level education for children and ignore higher education, college and university. Others offer college programs but fail to expand their vision to a faculty-based concept which could be a real alternative to that of conventional universities.

In fact, lots of instructors, teachers, professors, pedagogues, psychologists, and neuroscientists continue to lament the lack of real progress on the education front. Apart from the exceptions that only confirm the rule, the system does not show real signs of change and after two and half centuries since Rousseau's 'Emile' we are still here debating the same or similar issues he pointed out in his treatise. The above-cited cases remain confined to personal attempts at change and which do not always succeed, or do at best in small and few private schools or universities. Flip teaching and LdL remain far from being accepted methods that could begin to replace the outdated and encrusted teaching style. Khan Academy lectures are still elementary, not at real university levels. MOOCs have had a measure of success, with a small percentage of those who subscribe to a course effectively ending up with a degree. This is understandable, since there are not many institutions that recognize attendance on online courses. Why should students invest time in something their university will ignore? Of course, the process will need time to develop itself, but online learning is no longer a novelty. It has existed now for about two decades, and has not so far met the expectations of potential beneficiaries.

Professors still 'lecture'. Why? By the way, where does the word 'lecture' come from? Once upon a time, before Gutenberg's invention of the press in 1439, books were not printed but could be copied only by handwriting. They were still an extremely expensive good and were available only to the rich and to clerics. For students attending classes in what would become the first universities (mostly these were monks in monasteries), there were no textbooks, which would have been something they couldn't afford anyway. The only way to learn something from books was to attend the lecture of someone (the 'professor', a term which comes from the Latin 'profiteri' and means 'the one who speaks forwards') who read the only book available in front of a class. Upon the invention of the press and the cheap availability of books, not to mention the advent of digital media which made access almost free for all, this method of transmitting knowledge has become completely anachronistic. And yet, this tradition has been passed on to modernity, without substantial change or adaptation. After over six centuries, we are still 'lecturing'!

This example of humanity's stubborn and extreme resistance to change may also have something to do with the fact that, while the above-mentioned approaches contain a substance of truth, they might still miss something fundamental.

There have been improvements in education, of course, but only at the margins, and not in its fundamental nature where the paradigm still hasn't changed. The feeling persists that we are still scraping the surface, and haven't found the essence, the unifying principle.

Homeschooling and unschooling

Homeschooling, also known as 'home education', is that kind of education in which parents opt to educate their school-aged children at home rather than at a public or private school. Parents themselves take over the education of their children as teachers and tutors. Contrary to common belief, this is a form of education practice of which was and remains allowed in most Western countries. There are notable exceptions, however, like Germany or Sweden, where it is illegal. In some other countries, it is only a small peripheral phenomenon, but is nevertheless firmly anchored in their respective Constitutions, like in Italy. Homeschooling has a fairly widespread acceptance in the U.S., Canada, and the U.K.

Homeschooling is nothing new. In fact, it is the oldest form of child education, first practised by noble and rich families, who enlisted professional teachers for the private education of their children. Only privileged classes could afford this, while most of the middle and lower classes had to continue to subsist in ignorance and poverty. This was one of the reasons State-funded schools came into being. Their large-scale introduction in the 19th century in most of Europe opened up the system to all the strata of society. In this sense, compulsory school attendance played an invaluable role in uplifting the literacy of the masses which became the primary driving factor for a worldwide industrial and commercial growth. Homeschooling never quite died out, but became at that point an educational practice that only wealthy families maintained, and it survived also among those who preferred to educate their children according to religious precepts. For this reason, it was and still is connected until today to a somewhat negative connotation, as something that only the elites can afford, eventually even with a religious sectarian background.

However, this is by far no longer the case. In the last decades, an increasing number of families returned to homeschooling practices. Nowadays, most choose to educate their children at home not for religious motives or because of a financial privilege (quite the contrary turned out to be true, especially in the US: it is the most educationally disadvantaged strata that opt for this alternative), but because of their dissatisfaction with the traditional educational system, the same kind of dissatisfaction that we are reviewing here. Even though rules and restrictions differ from country to country, and may differ from region to region within a given country, it is a viable option for parents to keep their wards away from traditional school structures and homeschool them, where this not illegal. This option is seen to be experiencing a vigorous revival. Moreover, the homeschooling movement grew with the advent of the Internet which allowed for an easy and fast networking between like-minded parents and children.

However, traditional homeschooling maintains the conventional structured education of a school. It essentially transfers the authority of the teacher to one or both of the parents, and the location to the family domicile. Furthermore, the teaching carried out still follows the pedagogical concepts that drive the practices of the state school or the private school, and it still adheres to the curriculum and subject matter and set of tests that the state-controlled authority has developed. It is still top-down, adult-to-child teaching, the young learner still being told what to learn, and how and when. While homeschooling may achieve a large measure of independence from state-controlled education, it does not necessarily guarantee freedom of expression or of choice to the child. This still remains the parent's exclusive privilege.

'Unschooling' is a concept that dates back to the 1970s. It goes a step further away from the conventional notion of school-based education than homeschooling, in that it would have the child-learner free even from any form of control from their parents in the matter of learning. Unschooling is, in other words, characterized by the absence of a formal system of instruction with a curriculum and syllabus to go through according to a timetable, but allows children a self-directed learning where they are immersed in a community and environment (eventually, preceded by a transition period from school which, within the unschooler's culture, is also called 'deschooling'). Unschoolers are free to play as long as they wish, are encouraged to pursue their interests and self-direct their learning path.

This raises some pertinent questions and doubts. In a society where a standardized formal instruction has dominated and has been accepted almost without hesitation in both the public and the private school sectors for almost two centuries, it is hard to believe that children would want to learn, would be able to self-direct and self-discipline, and would be able to assume responsibility, all without authoritarian adult oversight. How can children learn reading, writing, doing maths, acquire a new language, etc., if they were to play all day? How will they be able, once they are grown up, to get a job without a degree and a formal course of training? What about their social skills? Will they be able to relate to others in their community, at their workplace, if they have never had to follow the rules of a collective like all the other kids in a classroom? Will they be able to develop the psychological resilience they will need in later life to withstand the hardships and pains of life?

The list of fears and prejudices is long. In fact, it is usually fear and unknowingness that dissuade most parents from taking this educational approach for their children. Even progressive-minded parents, who might eventually ponder the homeschooling or unschooling option, usually stay clear of this idea out of fear, criticism, and external social pressure. The path of conventional education is socially accepted, and does not need justifications and is less affected by uncertainties.

Modern research shows, however, that such fears are based on prejudices that have no basis in reality. For example, Peter Gray conducted several studies on unschoolers. His thesis is that *"children come into the world with instinctive drives to educate themselves"*. (72)

A survey in 2003 didn't find any evidence that homeschooling and even unschooling may cause any of the harm alluded to above. On the contrary, while in the minds of many school children the word 'learning' is associated with a sense of frustration and lack of freedom, unschoolers in particular showed better attitudes towards learning, suggesting improved psychological and social well-being for the children and increased closeness, harmony, and freedom for the whole family. (78) A great majority of former unschoolers had pursued some form of higher education and were gainfully employed as adults pursuing a wide range of jobs and careers, especially in the creative arts or as entrepreneurs. (79) Other studies show that the academic outcomes of homeschooled students who enter a medium-sized doctoral institution possess higher American College Testing (ACT) scores, grade point averages (GPAs), and graduation rates when compared to traditionally-educated students. (80) Other sources confirm that homeschoolers do not suffer socialization problems, as many fear. (81)

Many famous historical statesmen and personalities of culture were homeschoolers: George Washington, Theodore Roosevelt, and several other US presidents; composer Wolfgang Amadeus Mozart; physicists Erwin Schrödinger or Ernst Mach; inventor Thomas Edison. Living homeschooled personalities include Palmer Luckey, founder of virtual reality hardware enterprise Oculus VR; American singer and actress Selena Marie Gomez; and Arran Fernandez, a mathematician who became Senior Wrangler at Cambridge University, aged 18 years—just to mention some. (82)

To some these facts might look surprising and hard to believe. But, after all, a child does not learn to walk, or learn the mother tongue from a teaching process occurring in a classroom. A child learns this spontaneously, interacting with his parents, by imitation, and by playing with other children. The common belief that all this must abruptly change from the age of primary school onwards, is flawed. It is a tradition which has its roots in a historical development of humankind, but no scientific basis exists which indicates the opposite.

Moreover, according to Gray, children mostly educate themselves and learn the most valuable lessons with other children, away from adults. (83) Constant monitoring and supervision is detrimental for a child's healthy and natural development. And yet, this is precisely what modern society and educational institutions are increasingly promoting, especially with all-day schools. Gray summarizes: *"By increasing the amount of time spent in school, expanding homework, harping constantly on the importance of scoring high on school tests, banning children from public spaces unless accompanied by an adult, and replacing free play with adult-led sports and lessons, we have created a world in which children are almost always in the presence of a supervisor, who is ready to intervene, protect, and prevent them from practicing courage, independence, and all the rest that children practice best with peers, away from adults. I have argued elsewhere ((84), (85)) that this is why we see record levels of anxiety, depression, suicide, and feelings of powerlessness among adolescents and young adults today."* Gray also laments that children suffer a chronical 'play deficit'. A gradual reduction of children's opportunities to play and free time due to longer school days goes hand in hand with the increase of childhood mental disorders. But without the freedom to play children are denied a fundamental and natural right and mean of development which, over the years, has led to more anxiety and depression, lack of empathy and a decline of social skills. (86)

Unschooling sets a new educational paradigm, in the sense that it gets rid of any formal school system and is primarily based on trust. The trust in the child's potentialities and the confidence that children are able to find out what their own innate talents are and to take up responsibility. Not an easy act of faith in a world that has always thought and practised education on the opposite premises. But the fact that an increasing number of parents and pedagogues are now slowly but steadily accepting this possibility and practise it in different forms, is a sign of our times which will further develop in the coming years.

Big psychological and cultural hurdles have still to be overcome until this can become an established and normal fact in our society. It is still a deeply engraved conviction that children are not capable of teaching themselves and taking up responsibility for their own education. In most of our social structures, this is hard to see and believe, since they, the children, have never been allowed to do this, and therefore usually lose their innate ability for self-directed learning in their first years. They unlearn how to learn, so to speak. This in turn is taken as evidence which supposedly proves the contrary, and the vicious circle of prejudices and accustomed thought patterns reinforces itself. Take a tiger that has always lived in a cage, and set it free in a savanna. It will no longer be able to hunt and nourish itself and quickly starve to death. Should we therefore classify the tiger as a vegetarian sloth?

Another common criticism is that homeschooling and unschooling, particularly the latter, may not be the appropriate educational paths for every child and adolescent. According to this point of view, those children who are able to learn and teach themselves are only a tiny minority, a handful of 'geniuses' who will forever remain a marginal phenomenon. Now the question is: where do we know this from? How can we know this if children are almost never offered seriously the opportunity to demonstrate the contrary? Whatever the weighty arguments for the continuance of the prevailing authoritarian, top-down teaching system, it is my belief that it is grossly unfair to ban and outlaw homeschooling and unschooling. And the real point is that, even if that is the case and if many still may need a top-down authoritarian education which tells them what, when and how, and learn things according to a pre-determined timetable and curriculum without being allowed to learn how to become self-responsible, this can't be a good reason to ban and eventually also forbid by means of a state law, home- and unschooling for those (few or many) who instead are able to self-direct their learning path and are capable of educating themselves without coercions.

Not only is present-day Germany at the forefront of industrial and economic achievements, but is globally respected for the autonomy she has accorded to her social and civil-rights institutions that are often taken as exemplars by societies worldwide. It is therefore with considerable dismay that advocates of homeschooling and unschooling view the retrograde measure the country has taken in banning and illegalizing them. While in most modern democratic countries homeschooling is allowed in one or the other form, in Germany any form of homeschooling is strictly illegal. Historically, the interdict is a throwback to a law instituted by Adolf Hitler in 1938. The Third Reich considered the education of the child as falling under State jurisdiction, and not a matter of choice for the parents, even less so for the child: the parents (the theory went) had no time or the skills to do the teaching, and the child, of course, was unable to learn and develop without adult help—and the close supervision such as only the classroom could provide!

At the times of Nazi Germany this was an excuse that served well to prepare society to become fit for a globalized warfare. Nowadays, compulsory school attendance may serve as a tool to prepare the masses for a globalized version of commercial competitiveness. Germany was and is a commercial superpower, and a well-structured and organized form of school education imposed on all would be meant to serve the nation's interest. This dogma remains firmly rooted in the minds of most Germans as a self-evident, almost-natural pedagogical doctrine accepted without question by most. Remember, the Kingdom of Prussia was among the first countries in the world to introduce compulsory primary education. Now, this does not come without a cost, and at the individual level it leaves its scars. There is less and less time for the free development of individual skills, passions, and potentialities of the individual. German child rank worldwide as having the lowest appreciation of going to school. (87) Those families who want to practice homeschooling or unschooling are forced to emigrate if they want to avoid problems with the Government Office for Youth Welfare, and eventually juridical reprisals up to the worst-case scenario of child withdrawal by the authorities.

Things may change as time passes by and are actually very dynamic. On one side, recently, more restrictive measures have been re-enacted in some countries. In Italy and France, children that have been taught at home are subjected again to regular compulsory state school exams. In Germany instead, where homeschooling isn't allowed anyway, a growingly strong movement is striving to re-introduce the right of parents to teach their children at home. The same movement also offers legal assistance to school refusers (about 300,000 in Germany alone) and promotes forms of alternative education. (88)

What is at stake however, is not only the fate of a nation, but the entire educational and psychological wellbeing of the next generations worldwide. The spontaneous renaissance of homeschooling and the rise of the unschooling paradigm is a sign and a message. People feel a basic dissatisfaction towards schools and the standard educational system. These are a symptom and a reaction which searches for alternative solutions and tries to escape a repressive and outdated conception of education.

Now, is it possible that a model of education such as unschooling may be the last step in our march for the liberation of the spirit from the bonds of a standardized concept of education which pretends to be good for all? As we have already said, no model is good for all. Conventional schools based on an authoritarian concept of education might remain the appropriate learning environment for many also in the future. Private schools like Montessori or Waldorf might continue to play their role in society too. Homeschooling or unschooling might be another option which works well for others. The question is not which systems have to be abolished and replaced by another institution which claims to represent the ultimate truth, but whether new conceptions must be allowed to grow and take their place in a modern and continuously changing society besides those present ones serving a part of the coming generations. This is not a plaidoyer for the elimination of conventional state schools. It is a proposal which envisages an approach different to the conventional one, and yet desires to coexist peacefully with it. The coming decades will be characterized by generations where many children may no longer wish to be taught and directed without their consent.

Homeschooling and unschooling might be an answer for many, and at any rate it should be allowed and regulated in every civilized nation which claims to respect civil rights. Consider the serious consequences of an obstinate refusal to recognize these alternative forms of free expression!

While unschooling can be a first step in thinking out of the box, it can't be considered the last rung of the ladder of the development of a new idea which envisages an efficient learning community capable of forming free spirits who are expected to become grown-up personalities also at a professional level. The idea of letting children free to play when and how they want is fine, but does not fulfil their desire to learn things at a higher level of sophistication. Going into the woods and experiencing nature is indeed an essential ingredient for a healthy psychological and physical growth of the child which our modern society underestimates but, if we stop there, this alone can't lead to a high-level education. Learning alone at home complex and intellectually more challenging subjects from books or videos, or with internet research and eventually following online courses, can play an important role too, but is still insufficient to trigger the real learning process which can be experienced by project-oriented team work and a real research environment where experienced instructors can help along a learning path. Unschooling can be a point of departure, not that of arrival. It still lacks of some fundamental ingredients which are typical of a living learning community which wants to prepare itself for the highest achievable professional skills. While for some, homeschooling and unschooling in their present format might be sufficient, sooner or later others will feel the necessity to organize a free, self-determining and open learning community which conceives of infrastructures and an organization which will retain some aspects of a conventional school and is capable of preparing them for high-level college and university educational skills. Or to put it in other words: don't us let throw the baby out with the bathwater!

Most unschoolers object that, if one desires to acquire a higher degree of education, eventually with a certificate, anyone is free to do so by attending the present structures, that is the high schools and college. But this forces one again to be pressed into the very same learning environment which a free-progress learner is supposed to avoid. In some countries, folk high schools exist which prepare adults to attain academic degrees. But these are usually very limited and are just courses which prepare people as 'external students' to an examination of a school or academia. Not much more. These learning environments have no marks of FPE like the one we would like to propose here.

The democratic schools education paradigm

Perhaps the most interesting and relevant case, which might prove to be an inspiration potentially leading to a future FPE community for higher education might be the so-called democratic schools. Their origin can be found in the Summerhill school. In 1921, A. S. Neill, a Scottish educator, founded the Summerhill School, in Leiston, England. It was the first of the pioneering projects of a model that would later be followed worldwide, a model which envisages schools as a self-governing community and a place where children are free to choose their activities. Neill was light years ahead of his times, and his school concept remained an isolated example for about half a century.

Later, a similar concept was initiated in the 1960s by Daniel Greenberg with the 'Sudbury Valley Schools'. (89) These models provide a school environment where no one is forced to learn, and there are no grades, tests, or classes: children play and learn altogether without being organized in age groups. Democratic-school education is based on ideals in which democracy is both a goal and a method of instruction, and fosters self-determination as well as the values of justice, respect, and trust. In these schools, children are left free to choose if they want to learn maths, cook, or just play football. Students are set at the same level of teachers. A democratic school has no hierarchies; it is a community of equals. Self-determination, freedom, and democratic values are as important as responsibility, respect, justice and trust. School administration is regulated by means of democratic procedures and is run by the children and instructors together. Even though they may each be inspired by a somewhat different conception of democratic education, there are actually hundreds of democratic schools throughout the world which are inspired by the Summerhill School or Sudbury Valley Schools models. This is still a tiny number compared to the number of conventional or state schools, but their presence is growing.

Despite their name, democratic schools have almost nothing in common with what people mean by a 'school'. There are no classrooms, no subdivisions into age groups in grades, no fixed curricula or timetables, and in principle everyone is allowed to do nothing at all or play all the time instead of learning to read, write, do maths, etc. The pedagogical concept is in many respects much more like that of the unschooler ideal. What distinguishes a democratic school from a more or less spontaneously organized unschooler community is that in a democratic school students meet daily at a learning place where they come together physically inside an infrastructure (the 'school') which eventually organizes also learning courses and different kinds of educational activities. Life inside the democratic school is regulated too. It is not a chaotic environment without rules where everyone can trample on others without consequences. Children learn to connect their own freedom with rules and responsibilities towards the collective. There is an administrative body made up of all students and staff members that regulates all of the school's rules, hires and fires staff members, decides about the purchases, establishes committees, etc.

As for unschooling, many have severely criticized the democratic education ideal. How can children learn to read and write if they are allowed to do all the day what they want? Can children really self-direct their education without the adults intervening? What will happen when they are grown-up adults, and have not been forced to learn math, science, history, and/or literature and are not prepared well in advance to take exams and get certificates? Life is not a bowl of cherries. When do they learn to deal with its hardships? Won't these children later end up as ignorant, antisocial, and unemployable tramps?

These are legitimate questions which, however, reality answered all negatively. Facts, experience on the ground, research, and decades of generations of children attending democratic schools have demonstrated that they all learned to read and write, developed intellectual skills, do not demonstrate anti-social behaviours, and had no difficulty in being hired and in performing a job as well as any 'normal' citizen who attended regular schools.

Many unschoolers, or the supporters of the unschooling ideal, however do not accept the Summerhill or Sudbury Valley School education model either because, first of all, they are private schools, and as such are not funded (or are underfunded) by the state, which means that parents inevitably have to pay for school tuitions. Moreover, while in most countries democratic schools are tolerated, this is frequently made subject to some forms of restriction by the state, in effect diminishing the democratic ideal itself. For example, while, in principle, the democratic school ideal does not ask for compulsory attendance, in practice in some countries or regions daily attendance according to a strict timetable is compulsory because this is demanded as a necessary condition for recognition by the state authorities.

At any rate, in my opinion, the unschooling model, as also the practice of democratic education in democratic schools, still lacks a fundamental ingredient: a clearer vision, formulation, and understanding of how a free-progress system of higher education could be organized. The path from high school to university is, for unschooler as for democratic school students, not much different than that of any other conventional school student. There is no democratic or FPE concept for high school and university levels. Unschoolers who would like to acquire the skills and knowledge of a Ph.D. in some subject have to force themselves back in the good old system or to learn it all by themselves in solitary confinement behind a monitor following online courses. There are no learning places and structures where to meet with like-minded students and practise freely according to a free-progress ideal. Democratic schools rarely project themselves beyond a primary and secondary education level. After that, students in a democratic school who would like to attend university must join conventional high schools or be prepared, with the help of a mentor, to sit external exams for acquiring the standard college degree. There is no such thing as a Summerhill or a Sudbury Valley University. The circle of the democratic ideal is still not closed, even not in theory. Still rare are those who envisage a free-progress education beyond childhood. Lots of 'new' and 'free' schools are founded all over the world, and all are supposed to foster a free and democratic development for children from kindergarten to secondary school, but almost no thoughts go to the students in high school and college who are suffering the consequences of a still authoritarian mechanical and close-minded pedagogy which still dominates universities. Students in high school and college are left alone to their destiny, and are not allowed to attend any alternative form of higher education. Unschooling or democratic schools were the first necessary steps towards the liberation of the soul from the bondages of a repressive pedagogical concept, but if we do not go beyond the infancy of this new paradigm, there can't be no real new educational revolution. We will still continue to run endlessly in a hamster wheel wondering why it is that everyone is dissatisfied with education as it is practised. And nothing changes, generation after generation.

Rediscovering the true spirit of education

"The illiterate of the 21st century will not be those who cannot read and write, but those who cannot learn, unlearn, and relearn."

Alvin Toffler

Humanizing education

Once it is established that the current paradigm of pedagogical and didactical learning, working, and research is outdated, and no longer serves the needs of a modern society, the question would be: what should the alternative paradigm look like? There are two facets, two approaches in dealing with learning, research, and the advancement of culture generally. The first approach is to insist on the idea that we need even more skilled leaders, fundraisers, and managers who are able to direct large research programmes and groups of teachers, professors, and scientists. This envisages a huge, well-organized managerial system that pressures people to produce results quickly and in conformity with preset specifications. This paradigm does not envision pursuit of knowledge for its own sake. The second possibility, in contrast, might be a somewhat less ordered, nonlinear, and unpredictable process, which, however, should rediscover the ancient human impetus to understand nature, the drive to free, independent and creative thinking, the spirit of the natural philosopher who pursues the freedom to develop his/her own research programme, the inspired musicians or contemplative artists, and which liberates everyone's intellectual independence and potential independently of its possible applications. The social, cultural, and economic future of humanity will depend on the choice we make today.

True, in this market-driven world of ours, the latter alternative may sound too romantic. But didn't modern society bet too much on the former? After all, where did the great minds that transformed the world materially come from? From schools and universities where they learned only the real-world practice preparing them for their future jobs, or from institutions that also foster theoretical approaches of pure thought, like philosophy and humanistic practices like music and the arts? How could it be that a genius like the German writer, poet, and scientist Johann Wolfgang von Goethe never went to school at all? Or, just to mention another interesting homeschooling case, the father of André-Marie Ampère kept his son far from formal schooling, allowing him to educate himself instead, and Ampère went on to become one of the greatest physicists of the 17th century. It is an established fact that most inventors, geniuses, and not rarely corporate leaders too, either did not attend schools which focus exclusively on a technical apprenticeship aimed solely at attaining a professional certificate, or even did not go to school at all. It may be argued that they were geniuses just because they could make it nevertheless, even without attending a standard school system. But are we sure that truth does not go the other way around? The choice to let them be free to learn by themselves was the key, and they might never have become known if they had been forced into schools with strict paths and curricula.

What is really needed in schools and in the field of pre-college and university education at this historical stage of the scientific, technological, and human development is the freedom to ask one's own questions, and having the time to do that, without the danger of not being able to make a living. Nowadays, we begin by injecting already-established knowledge into the child's brain, but do not exercise him/her by asking questions that should lead them to that knowledge. We may call this 'top-down teaching'. Instead, it should be the other way around: 'bottom-up learning' that starts from the individual's questions and that leads, along a lifelong learning process, to new insights and knowledge. Our concept of education is still too much focused on the choices to be made today in order to get a degree that will guarantee a job tomorrow. The inner drive towards one's own realizations, aspirations, spontaneous questioning, and creativity are still too much subordinated to the impossible guess of what a decade-away job might look like, and children and students are forced to learn in order to be able to make a living in a future competitive, global market. We haven't still learnt the lesson that predictions of this type rarely turn out to be correct anyway. Moreover, jobs are usually about the production of material goods. Therefore, from childhood onward we are told by our society and learning system to focus on the external world, on the empiric data, on the strictly material knowledge and experience. But no time is allowed to listen to ourselves, to investigate our own inner depth, to search for the inspiration and passion which comes from within.

The exclusive concentration on a few intellectual directions to the exclusion of others, retracting the support to individuals working on their own approaches, has led us to a cultural environment incapable of going beyond the status quo. This state of affairs, which is more or less consciously and vaguely felt by students and potential bright minds, has led many to resign themselves entirely to their careers, and nowadays are no longer working in the field their heart was longing for. At the other end of the line, most of those who got to the top of the scientific or academic hierarchy have become not scientists who manage research, but managers, politicians, bureaucrats, the only difference being that they have a degree in science. Most managers are not in their position because of their professional merits, or for their particular achievements, but mainly because of the egocentric driving power which is based on an unusual vital force. For them, despite their officially stated intentions, the project of the industry, of the sales department, or the research centre they are working for, functions for their own career promotion, in order to climb up a power hierarchy. It is not a priority for them to create products or knowledge that fosters the progress of society as something which should serve the interests of a collective wellbeing. This is so not because they are evil, but simply because the system in its essence intrinsically rewards egoism, and discourages any social conscience.

This principle is clearly visible in education, especially in higher education: most directors, chancellors, department heads, and group leaders of academic institutions are not original thinkers or creative geniuses who were promoted to a higher rank for their intellectual achievements, but are usually old-fashioned conservative close-minded people, who were able to propel themselves to a higher position since they possessed an unlimited desire and ambition for self-promotion, and a huge ego that is supported by an enormous amount of psychological energy. The more modest and less egocentric but much more creative mind is mostly ignored, and this latter character is precisely the type of personality which is devalued by the present system. I'm not talking of worldwide conspiracy theories. Quite the contrary: there is no physical person or group of persons that are controlling this state of affairs. It is an abstract system of written laws and bureaucratic regulations that has in its grip everyone of us (for the most part, however, unconsciously). It is a dictatorship without a dictator. And precisely for that reason it is difficult to become aware of it, since there is no physical person to blame, and yet the machine continues to churn.

New selection criteria must be found, where the person, the scholar, the scientist is chosen, not for their sterile scholastic preparation or selfishness, but for their ideas, ideals, aspirations, and passions. And even the actuality of the line of research they propose shouldn't be considered essential. Funding must not be granted to someone only because the line of research is actually considered the most trendy, but at least a part of it should be devoted to alternative, risky, and unconventional paths.

School classes and university courses should become more flexible, that is, they should be conceived first of all not just as a place where to acquire knowledge and solve problems. Amassing knowledge shouldn't be its main purpose or preoccupation. Nowadays, with the advent of the information age and the Internet, everyone who can read and write together with a minimum of IT skills is perfectly able to download every kind of information needed without the help of a teacher or professor. These are no longer key figures for information retrieval, whereas their function should be that of showing students how they can become able to find that knowledge on their own. Educational institutions should be a place where people learn to learn, and learn to ask questions, and learn what has to be learned by themselves, with the help of someone who is not an instructor, a trainer, or a drill sergeant, but a counsellor, a guide, a coach, a tutor, a mentor, an attendant who facilitates our own personal search for knowledge and self-unfoldment. Let us call this figure a 'learning mentor'. Children and students should no longer be treated as empty containers to be filled with intellectual notions. Ph.D.s, postdocs, and researchers should not be considered mere employees who have to obey orders passively and blindly.

Too much emphasis has been set on intellectual rigour, on mathematical perfection, on mechanical skills which are too exclusively focused on reproducing quickly specific tasks and by fast problem- solving with zero tolerance for failure. But a creative process rests on the freedom to fail in a system that abhors uniformity. A good problem-solver is someone who has learned to ask good questions first. How idiotic would sports be if it were to apply the same selection rules for marathoners and sprinters? It would be as idiotic as our present educational system based on standardized tests and quizzes. And, as Sir Ken Robinson uses to say: "We have developed a culture where mistakes are stigmatized". (90) In fact, every scientist who has some direct experience of participating in a research project, be it in a purely theoretical context, or by performing experiments in a laboratory, knows very well that most attempts to discover a new scientific truth have to first go through several failures. If you never fail, you are probably doing something wrong. That can only be due to the fact that you are not doing something new, original, innovative. An education that institutionalizes fear of failure is by definition a conservative and authoritarian system. It gave us lots of efficient executors indeed, but it also killed the spirit of the creative and curious thinker. In this kind of environment, the visionary, the 'seer', the intuitive thinker, the creative artist, the genuine talent, and the genius are naturally de-selected from the outset. Human beings are too diverse and complex to be enclosed in a single school or an academic educational approach that measures them with quantitative criteria that are rigidly uniform for all. There are a lot of diverse talents, approaches, and styles to be found in humankind. Still, most of the current schools and universities impose only one possible path. These institutions should open themselves to all the human characters: to the analytical, the intuitive, the artistic, the unconventional, the 'rebel' minds, etc.

We frequently hear people talking about the autonomy and freedom of science. But, in this regard, most research centres of today are the problem, not the solution. They look exclusively at the speed and precision of intellectual reproduction and potential for manufacture, hopefully with lots of papers published, and possibly added with good communication skills of the individual in order to keep high the image and prestige of the group or department. But motivation (intrinsic or extrinsic) is officially seen as secondary. A free-progress environment is necessary because there are several young students, or potential students, who feel the inner drive to explore the deeper meaning of things, who have an open and curious mind towards alternative approaches, who have great inspirations and aspirations that could serve the collective development of a nation, or even humanity as a whole. But, when they enrol in a college, they discover that there is no such thing as an opportunity to express themselves. Individual development is hampered. They are forced to repress their own inner potentialities, and are compelled to follow lines that are not their own. If they want to make a career, they have no other way out than sacrificing all to a study and professional path which has nothing to do with what their inner soul is longing for and with what their real destiny should be.

Many of these individuals are led to believe that there is something wrong with them, and fall prey to depression and stress, and finally abandon entirely the studies they had pursued for several years. Nowadays, those who perceive an urge to go beyond a mere analytical and superficial understanding of the physical world, those who want to focus on specific subjects because there is an inner drive to do so, must set aside these yearnings. They would like to progress and change and evolve, but are forced to inhibit and even suppress their own evolution.

Nowadays everyone is talking about 'excellence'. But what is excellence? Setting up highly selective institutions that bring together the 'best brains', and order them to do what is required from the top, like chickens in a henhouse? Every manager would deny this, and all unanimously would tell us that they look for creative and original thinkers. Facts on the ground are quite different. The typical modern managerial mindset appeals for more creative thinking and originality in schools, but does not allow it in its own entrepreneurial environment. Working under pressure and in multitasking is the motto and main pedagogical ideal of several top managers and academics, who continue to ignore the basic facts emerging from psychology and brain research which clearly tell us that this is the most counterproductive approach. This is a pedagogy that tells the what, when, and how of the job. Every attempt to put forward one's own ideas, projects or alternative approaches is seen as an irritating attempt to overthrow authority. Obviously, those in charge are always a bit disappointed that, despite having under their grip several people who eventually publish lots of scientific papers, still not many groundbreaking ideas emerge. There is a pressure which generates fear, anger, sadness, frustration, and ultimately hampers the emergence of a further consciousness in most individuals studying and working in industries or schools, universities and research centres. And, if things continue to go wrong, the pressure is enhanced. But it should become clear instead that the solution is not to persist in doing more wrong things. An entirely new approach is needed. Real excellence can come only from within. This awareness remains as alien to most teachers, academic figures and mangers today as it did in the past.

Integral education[2]

The industrial revolution and the tremendous success of the sciences, which led us to almost overwhelming technological progress and economic growth without parallels in human history, were the products of the age of enlightenment. It is mainly because of this movement of the 18th century, which draws its thought from the philosophy of the founders of modern science, like Galileo and Newton, that nowadays we can drive cars, use computers, transport ourselves throughout the world or communicate with a space probe at the edge of the solar system. The age of enlightenment allowed humanity to make a big leap forward and ultimately transformed our society.

However, this seemingly unstoppable material success of human reason and the marvelous power of scientific thinking have lured us into a belief system which has become a more or less unconscious, deeply engraved conviction: namely, that every problem can be solved only inside a strict rational and analytic thinking framework. Every institutional order must be organized according to purely mental rules. Every job and activity is worth pursuing if it serves a material purpose and every form of knowledge is

---

[2] The concept of an 'Integral Education' was largely inspired by the vision of Mirra Alfassa. Refer to the endnote of the book for more details.

true knowledge only if it can be falsified by science, as scientific truth has become the only possible truth. And, of course, every true education is that which teaches rational, analytic and logical thought processes, such as mathematics and science. This is because these are the skills which created our modern advanced industrial technological society and which allowed for all its practical material applications and utilitarian purposes. 'Learning' has become synonymous almost exclusively with mental activity, information retrieval and analysis, rational thinking, and analytic skills. The skills and growth of the emotional, physical, intuitive, creative and spiritual dimensions of the human being receive only scarce or secondary attention, if any. In our modern conception of education, learning is about learning to think, whereas learning through feeling, perceiving and intuition is an ability that we do not believe composes what we nowadays think that education in schools, colleges and universities should be. It remains a personal matter, at best.

The enlightenment and all its thought and philosophical movements were – and will remain – essential ingredients for the progress of the human race. However, it is time to reconsider it and recognize its limits. The human being is not only a thinking being. Our problems won't be solved only with scientific means. The challenges we must confront, even those of a technical nature, can't be addressed with technology alone. Our educational model, which fosters only the power of the mind while neglecting the other potential powers, skills and abilities of the child, is not only a limited form of education but also a dangerous one. There is too much emphasis in our society on analytic rigor, which leaves almost no room for other cognitive functions, such as intuition, feeling and inspiration.

In this regard, it might be instructive to rediscover Pestalozzi's approach, which conceived of the child's education from different perspectives as an integrated whole and which resulted from a synergy of different levels of existence. Physical, emotional, moral and ethical education was not subservient to intellectual education. 'Hands-on' learning was not considered less essential than 'mind-on' learning. He became known for his 'hands-heart-head' paradigm, which conceives of balanced physical, emotional and mental development, avoiding an exaggerated emphasis on one or the other levels. Love, feelings, matter and thought are equally part of the healthy development of our body, emotions and mind. The goal is to educate the whole without giving in to the temptation to favor too much or repress the parts. Music, drawing, painting or physical exercise were not considered less important than math or language. Pestalozzi's concept of knowledge is not reduced to an intellectual exercise applied to dry facts and data analysis, but is also an insight that arises from a lived experience and sensory perceptions. Real learning comes from one's own experience at all levels: mental, physical, emotional and spiritual. The moral powers of the heart, such as love, compassion or gratitude, should not be neglected, not even in classrooms. Living the environment in nature through direct experience of the senses is as important a central exercise as – if not more important than – any verbal learning based on books.

Pestalozzi lived in a society which is now two-and-a-half centuries removed from ours. Not everything must be accepted and integrated into our modern pedagogical concepts; some we might even reject and consider outdated. However, more than ever, this integrative fundamental principle remains real.

Education is a never-ending process. It lasts until the end of our lives. Precisely for this reason, it can't be reduced to school and college attendance alone. It must embrace all of a human's mental, physical emotional, intuitive and spiritual existence. Education should be a process of self-discovery by which the child becomes aware of all these planes and parts and learns to develop and use them consciously. It is about an 'integral education' that invites us to a more holistic perspective. An integral education is much more than a school which prepares a student for a future job. Physical education not only can prepare one for physical strength but can also teach moral values such as discipline, endurance, method and patience or suggest physical norms like correct hygiene and healthy eating habits. Emotional education – an aspect which is almost completely ignored in conventional schools – can help develop one's character and self-control, as well as enlarge us by encouraging us to develop feelings of love, beauty and compassion. The spiritual dimension must be discovered and disclosed by education as well. Questions about the meaning of life, about the purpose of our existence and about our true identity should not be dismissed as childish quests. To the contrary, they should be encouraged and nurtured. An intuitive education aims to develop intuition, inspiration, curiosity and higher cognitive faculties or skills. And, of course, in this integral vision, mental education has its place. However, it should proceed hand in hand with the other forms of education, without being regarded as the ultimate cognitional crone at the top of a pyramidal concept.

Therefore, what we need at this stage is a realization of how limited and restricted our concept of education is. We need a wider, all-embracing understanding of human nature. From there, we must draw our conclusions and proceed.

Acknowledging the soul factor

With this integral and integrative approach it is no longer difficult to recognize how even more important than contributing to financial security, education is expected to bring to the individual a means to achieve a degree of self-perfection, through a progression of consciousness. This can only happen if we discard our long-held and widely-accepted academic attitudes in favour of a new understanding of the human being. Instead of brilliant students, we must look for the living souls that feel the 'fire of progress'. Under the free-progress system, people align with themselves, students learn to align with their 'inner guidance system', and progress is guided by an inner inspiration, and is not subject to habits, conventions, or preconceived pedagogical ideas or theories.

There is now an increasing awareness that most of our top-down educational systems do not foster creativity and freedom, and, in fact, hamper the genius and the intuitive thinker. An important acknowledgement, which however, as we have seen, isn't new. Many are realizing the misalignment between the ideals we have about liberating a new spirit and the everyday reality in primary and secondary schools. But, to the best of the author's knowledge, there are at present only sporadic attempts to look for concrete ways for this misalignment to be repaired. A bottom-up approach for a fully-fledged professional higher education is also overdue. Once we have acknowledged the lack of freedom for creativity in schools and colleges, what should the next practical step be?

Of course, we hear about reforms, need for change and new laws, and appeal to those in charge and responsible for educating new generations to change their mind, and take action. But so far not much has changed in these respects. Why? Sure, shifts take time to take effect. This shift is still in progress and yet not complete. But the number of people who woke up and realized the limits and intrinsic failure of the actual system has grown enormously in the last years. And yet the very same people working, teaching, and conducting research in these institutions seem unable to change anything. If they are part of the same academic system, why do they not make a difference? There must be something missing.

The point is that any attempt to reform education, without a profound understanding of human nature and the uniqueness of the individual in his/her multi-dimensional spiritual aspects, will never be able to go far enough, and will always contain the seed of an unconscious mechanical reformulation of the past. For example, intuitions or revelations are considered interesting side effects at best, but the higher states of consciousness of the seer or intuitive genius are not deemed worthy to be nurtured and exercised. In this new view, the only real teacher, or professor, is the inner soul, with its guidance, where the intuition of truth can come only from within and above. We should accept that every human being is not only unique and indispensable, but has a mission, an inner plan, or existential programme listed in its soul. And it is this inner soul with its existential programme that must have the central command and priority. A school or university may provide all the structures, technology, teaching, and assistance to develop all of our psychological planes, but real integral development will continue to elude us unless we submit to the guidance of this sacred inner presence in us. In other words, the ideal of freedom and progress of the soul and the inner consciousness is more urgent than the preoccupation with acquiring skills and intellectual knowledge. Not only is the latter less important than the former but the latter can't follow integrally without the former. Therefore, the priority at present is to identify how to create the practical conditions that could lead to this inner freedom and progress in our worldly existence. Beyond an abstract declaration of intent, there haven't been many proposals so far for the high school, university, and research levels.

Hi-tech classrooms, pedagogical research, or new didactical methodologies are all fine, but finally, only an education with a soul, and especially a learning for and through the soul, will lead us towards real reform. We need an education for children, an academy for undergraduates and graduates, and research centres which follow the call of the spirit. If people feel increasingly the pressure of stagnation and sameness, this is because these are aspects alien to their soul which develops with change and variation, and in diversity in unity. If nowadays we have to complain about a lack of creativity, this is because the present system is intrinsically designed to hold imprisoned our inner being which naturally tends to freedom, curiosity, passion, inspiration, and aspiration. If there are so many who don't know what to do with their lives, this is a consequence of the deafness that our society imposes on the inner voice of the soul which knows better than anyone else what our mission is. If, despite all the technological means and material progress around us, we still feel a lack of space for intuition and inspiration, and the number of geniuses who made paradigmatic shifts is woefully low, this is due to the fact that other levels of consciousness of the intuitive mind are not considered, or at best only unconsciously and vaguely recognized. It is for decades that we have been hearing about the great advantages of multidisciplinarity, but an ever-increasing specialization that dissects and particularizes remains the only possible path, because the intuitive understanding which is naturally holistic and flexible, and tends to an all-encompassing view, is meticulously expunged in favour of purely mechanistic and analytic approaches. After all, the word 'university' itself comes from the Latin word 'universitas', noun of 'universus', which means 'all turned into one', or 'the whole', implying a universal knowledge as an interdependent whole. Instead, today we have 'multi-' or 'poli-versities', flattened by 'uniformity'. In contrast, it is the ideal of an FPU to recover the real and original meaning of university. Therefore, revelations, innovations, the realization of dreams, and exceptional cognitive events still remain rare, and will remain so forever, if the institutions where new generations of scientists, philosophers, musicians, and artists pursue their activities continue to refuse to open themselves to the higher cognitive dimensions.

If technology alone were the key, why is it that, in this computer and Internet era of ours, with its enormous creative potential, we find ourselves in the middle of an educational crisis, and the most preferred activity of an apparently unmotivated youth is that of playing video games? Sure, online universities, computer networks, open online courses, new digital technologies, social network learning, original didactical tools, teaching strategies, computer animated graphics, etc., are all fine, and they will undoubtedly contribute to a new cultural renaissance, but they won't do the job of liberating fully the creative potential inside every one of us. If the role of technology is emphasized too much, it will remain blind to the needs of the human spirit and its potential for advanced knowledge.

We must look further afield, much further afield, towards an understanding of the human psyche as an entity that does not follow a system of conformity and uniformity, but as a soul in evolution, intrinsically unpredictable and aiming at unexpected novelty and multiplicity in diversity. The human soul can't be grown, nurtured, and controlled like a machine, but must be acknowledged as a process inherent in life. A living soul is not an abstract concept, and isn't a mechanistic entity that can be measured with tests and grades, and its skills and abilities commanded and controlled by a set of lectures, eventually adding the pressure of fear of failure. The human being has been pressed into such a machine gear for a long time, but, whether we like it or not, something in it wants to progress, to grow, to learn, and will sooner or later break through its restraint and blow it up.

[3] The core assumption of an FPE paradigm is that everyone is a soul in progress – a being in evolution, a divine spark and seed that has the potential to grow and develop. This evolution and development of that

---

[3] The following four paragraphs are a revised transcript from (102).

divine element already inside every one of us is, however, something highly individualized and personal. In fact, it is futile to believe that there exists a universal formula which sums up all the skills and what is supposed to be the general knowledge and culture that is supposedly good for all and that should be crammed into a school or university curriculum. Everyone's individual interests, skill and strengths are an expression of the soul's need for self-expression and the desire to evolve through experience. However, these inner needs are diverse, even divergent, between people and the time and rhythm at which each child (or adult) learns something are extremely different. This is not because someone is better than or inferior to someone else, but because our inner being has a wisdom of its own and knows much better than we do what is good or bad for us and whether one thing or another must be learned and whether this or that must be accomplished quickly or slowly. It is a matter of 'soul-growth', so to speak. FPE is about allowing the soul to shine by revealing its true aspiration of action in the manifestations. Conventional education, instead, veils or even entirely blocks this light, replacing its true purpose with an artificial external goal.

That's the reason why preconceived curricula with deadlines and precise roadmaps intended to fit all, inside a structure that treats everyone as if we are all the same (behind a mask of false democratic values), can't work. An education that puts us into a strictly artificial age-structured classroom environment where the system tells you what to do, as well as when and how to do it, is a deeply unnatural and unhealthy way of learning. It refuses to recognize our inner being, the potential of our inner individual source and sacrifices it on the altar of a collective machinery. The result is that we hamper and suppress a natural inner evolution which must conform the inner to the outer.

According to an FPE view, instead, we are embodied souls who have an intrinsic and natural tendency and necessity to evolve by a self-expression in the manifestation. Here, each one of us proceeds along our own highly personalized way, according to what we really are, from the inside out and not vice-versa as is done nowadays. That's the real Latin meaning of education, 'educere', which tells us to 'draw something out' of the soul, not to put something in it. It is about the soul stepping forward, not about the person who must be pressed backwards to conform to external conditions. That's why only a soul-centered and soul-growth education which allows for self-expression and the self-unfoldment of that soul-being can work. If our mindset changes and allows for an educational paradigm that is sufficiently flexible, having the plasticity to adapt to each individual needs, it can succeed in creating a different humanity which is capable of more creativity, originality and critical thinking, and, as a side effect, more empathy, compassion and tolerance.

An education focusing on work and money is the exact opposite of that. It starves the soul and tries to impose outside conditions on an inner psychic world. It prioritizes the interest of big industry and the financial world and sacrifices individual potential. This exaggerated emphasis on purely intellectual skills is toxic. That's why children should, first of all, play, as modern psychology is now rediscovering, because that is what contributes to healthy growth, as well as to the development of intellectual capacities. Forcing children to engage in intellectual exercises too early and to an excessive extent means repressing their real souls, their true inner beings, and consequently making them aggressive or depressive – or, in the worst case, causing them to develop mental illnesses. Grades and tests have the function of forcing children to learn precisely those skills necessary to make money in the present economic and financial world. However, this systematically suffocates the soul's evolution and needs. Ultimately, the soul craves self-expression. However, it can't achieve this because it isn't allowed to do, as it must serve that collective machinery. Meanwhile, children fundamentally love to learn and seek knowledge. Why? Because it is an intrinsic property of everyone's soul, the inner being; it is part of human nature. In a certain sense, nothing can be taught, as learning is an active process which leads to a self-directed acquisition and cannot be imposed. Learning reveals itself as a 'dis-covery' of something which was already present in us. The role of the so-called 'teacher' should be only to help us reveal what was already innate.

Therefore, FPE is about the freedom of the soul to progress through a soul-centered, soul-growth education in which the role of the teacher is not to teach at all but to assist, coach and help in this process of growth. The teacher's role is also to create the outer, down-to-earth infrastructural and administrative conditions that allow this process to take place freely, without hindrances, so that children, teenagers, students and adults alike can express the potentials they all have inside.

In brief: there won't be any new reform, regulation, or technological means that will lead education to a real renewal if the inner individual human dimension isn't acknowledged, nurtured, and grown. It is all about the free progress of the soul which guides itself through a 'soul formation' and 'soul evolution'. The unifying principle is an evolving 'soul factor' of the human being. This will be key.

Towards liberation from ordinary education

Learning is a process of individual development and as such should become a basis for the free individual unfoldment and personal development as it is prescribed by one's inner potential. It is time to look further afield for an independent place where this type of free-progress approach in education can emerge and can serve a new kind of society. Not so much because there aren't people capable of giving effect to a free-progress approach in the present ordinary conventional schools and academia, but because the present educational system is intrinsically designed to refute this alternative since it is based on a machinery that appoints to the top of the hierarchy just those who are alien to this educational conception.

We would expect an institution to be guided by the best minds, for instance the best-performing students. But who are actually meant to be the 'best', especially in present schools and universities? All too frequently they are not those who have shown skills of creativity, originality, or intuition. They turn out, on the contrary, to be just those who managed to be best in adapting themselves to the preordered classical intellectual or political system, and those who were more successful than others in adjusting their character to a tradition-bound institution, and perform its assigned tasks faithfully. These individuals are rewarded for their loyalty, and will be those who climb up the ladder of the hierarchical structure. And from there they won't be able to do anything else than perpetuate the same system in its disguised appearances and different masks. It is inherent in their education and character, they can't do otherwise. If you are a sheep, you will always behave like a sheep, and once you will become the head of the flock, you will again maintain a system for sheep. Expecting a reform from inside of this environment is vain, it can't emerge, or if it does, it will take centuries. The economic and personal interests which stand in the way are much too powerful, the fear of change and innovation too strong, and a blind pragmatic conception of education itself much too deeply engraved in the mind of those who would have the power and the authority to make the needed changes happen. Why should someone call for a change or even elimination of something that promoted him to a dominant position? The pressure of a potential judgement from the system and the institutional environment (parents, colleagues, other institutions, politics, eventually even the media, etc.) is so strong that even the most powerful dean rarely dares to step outside the given conventional schemes. And to expect something from politics is even more unrealistic. Politicians are the guardians of the past, their job is to conserve and maintain what is.

There has never been, in all human history, a single example where new groundbreaking social and cultural reforms came from politicians without pressure from below. Their primary function has always been to preserve conformity and uniformity, never to progress. Why should it be otherwise this time? One has to stay instead completely out of the power hierarchies and political games, and offer directly an alternative system of knowledge acquisition as something that students can follow without any need to enrol in present academic institutions (even though student internship and exchanges should remain a normal practice), or to obey a prescribed curricular agenda suggested by governments or states.

Therefore, only a school and university which bases itself on the principles of a free progress of the inner being, which allows for an external expression and development of the true and genuine inner character, can offer a valid alternative, and the possibility to grow further. It is about building a self-determined learning community which fosters a free, self-designed progressive learning and a sounder and broader knowledge paradigm. A place where young people are not pushed into it, as they are nowadays, but one that pulls them to it. A great cultural concentration point where knowledge, timetables, curriculums, systems, etc. are not forced upon minds, but one that attracts minds by an intrinsic motivation. It is only in such a condition of an expanded freedom of expression that the human being can grow, flourish, and express itself. It will finally be the inner drive which will suggest the true way to follow. If this is not done, and so far it hasn't been, the rest can't follow.

In this respect a short digression might be useful to enlighten the deeper meaning of the above. In these times of globalization, enterprises like big science projects as also most industrial activities, are inevitably multidisciplinary. A huge 'cross-fertilization' between subjects and knowledges has grown exponentially in parallel with the expansion of the media and IT technologies. There is no longer an aspect of science that could be grasped entirely or a problem that could be solved without resort to a multidisciplinary perspective. As a typical example, one might think of the issue of climate change. This involves disciplines like, physics, chemistry, meteorology, agriculture, economics, politics, sociology, etc., which became all intertwined with an ever-increasing complexity. It is amply clear that future generations must learn to think and act with a global, multi- and inter-disciplinary approach. However, on the other side, every one of these single subjects alone has grown in an uncontrollable manner, especially with the advent of the digital era, and each of them has become so tremendously vast and complex that it is almost impossible for a single brain to oversee all the knowledge and to possess the skills that only one discipline requires. It questionable if it makes sense at all that young and inexpert minds should be forced to follow a true multidisciplinary education. What is really necessary is the ability of the individual to think from a multidisciplinary perspective and learn to act inside an interdisciplinary collaboration. But that won't come about from forcing students to learn a bit of everything or by amassing subject after subject in schools in the belief that it is still possible to acquire the foundations and basics in every subject. Unfortunately this is instead still the (more or less unconscious) idea and tendency today.

We still are attached to the chimera of the basic knowledge and the foundations a child must absorb. But the fact is that there is no longer such a thing. No human brain can learn all the basics and foundations of a single science, let alone that of a multidisciplinary science. Lots of school reforms and reshufflings of the curricula are desperately trying to keep pace with modern changes and technological and scientific progress. The extent of concepts, notions, and bookish knowledge that modern children and students are supposed to learn is growing exponentially, as is the pressure from many sides to impose one or the other subject as compulsory for all. Insisting on this direction won't work as long as this is practised inside a coercive system which owns it, instead of allowing a free choice between specialization and multidisciplinary and interdisciplinary learning. Such insistence will only exacerbate stress and depression symptoms in students. Interdisciplinary approaches could be encouraged, not imposed. Interdisciplinarity is the ever-present mantra among pedagogues and entrepreneurs and schools for decades, and yet a sense of dissatisfaction prevails. That won't and can't change, because it necessarily amounts again to a prescription of what children and students must learn instead of allowing for a freedom of choice. The attempt to instil multidisciplinary knowledge and skills against specialization isn't a better pedagogical approach than forcing the opposite specialized method of learning. If one or the other way of learning contradicts one's own existential programme, it can only produce harm or at best confusion or disinterest. If the soul longs for multidisciplinarity and we force on it specialization, that can't lead in a healthy direction. However, x the opposite is also true, and this is something we so frequently seem to forget.

At this stage, it is not only about finding funds for building new schools, universities, new laboratories, or about some new technology that is supposed to allow for more freedom and self-expression. Probably we are still not well enough aware of how deeply ideas about education with their roots mostly in the first educational reforms of the 19th century are engraved in our minds. Otherwise, we would not speak about reforming but about abolishing something. Could slavery and apartheid be 'reformed'? These things could not be ameliorated or regulated by better laws. They had to be abolished entirely. Was it morally conceivable to maintain child labour by making it more 'civilized'? Nobody would put it in these terms nowadays. Most would agree today that it has to be eliminated. After all, the Enlightenment did not arise from a reform of the Church's inquisition which controlled the culture and academia in the middle ages, and which imprisoned Galileo and burnt Giordano Bruno at the stake. It was a radical departure of traditional structures from the power of clerics, that ignited the scientific revolution in Europe. What is needed is not a reform but a departure from the stagnant establishment and a rebirth into a new and living existence.

One might object that comparing the actual educational system to past forms of slavery goes too far. But the real difference is not qualitative but experiential, and resides in the learning-slave effect. Slaves knew that they were slaves. Most of modern students and teachers are enslaved too, but we are so accustomed to the present system and take it so much for granted that it is the only and the most natural way to acquire knowledge and express expertise, that we have only a vague sense of being imprisoned by a mental construction. We may perceive an inner uneasiness and dissatisfaction, but we are still far from a full awareness of 'The Matrix'-like illusion this scenario represents. We don't even have an understanding of what a different approach to teaching and learning could be like. But a time will come when future generations will look back at our educational institutions as institutionalized forms of repression, and will view our present-day school system as being on the same moral level as we today judge child labour to be.

But what lay, and still lies, behind all of that resistance? Almost everyone agrees that something has to change, and yet nothing moves. In a certain sense, this is due to the fact that the present system works somehow. After all it produces many bright minds which, once trained and drilled, are capable of producing, building, manufacturing. And as long as our society can stand on its own feet with the conventional system of education, why should we criticize it and want to change it? I like to compare this reasoning to that of the smoker who knows all too well that this unhealthy habit might lead to death, but as long he feels healthy he will continue to smoke. When lung cancer is diagnosed, it will be too late, but there is something in the human nature that is passive, inert, and asleep that doesn't bother as long the situation does not collapse. There is something in us that likes to move only when a catastrophe takes place.

Behind the resistance to change was, and still is, there has been fear. The fear of losing power and wealth, the fear of innovation, the fear of the consequences of what a new concept and perception might bring. Nowadays, this fear expresses itself in the instinctive 'what if' mental and emotional reflex. What if we change this or that aspect of education? What if we switch from a generations-old system to a new and unexplored methodology? What if we spend money on a new pedagogical and didactical project of which the outcome is unpredictable? If things go wrong, we might have to justify our failures, we might lose our prestige, or we even might be fired. What if I send my children to a school that applies new methodologies which have never been tried out before?

Understandably, parents don't want pedagogues experimenting with their child like lab animals, and instinctively prefer to revert to the good old tested educational systems (what they probably do not know is that teachers do that routinely anyway, also in the present conventional school context). And so, even if a timid attempt at innovation surfaces from time to time, we feel nevertheless more comfortable maintaining everything as it is, and the system continues to hold its grip on our consciousness, perpetuating itself ad infinitum. Because finally, conservative, unreflective, fear-based, reflex driven thought patterns, that ultimately come from the survival mode of our reptilian brain are what unconsciously dictates these conservative actions.

This can be seen, for example, even in modern industrial and educationally advanced nations such as Germany. The attempt to reform a tripartite schooling system which categorizes, and consequently stigmatizes, 9– to 10–year-old children into 'good', 'average', and 'bad' ones, assigning them to the 'Gymnasium' school (those who are prepared for academics), the 'Realschule' (the middle class school, mostly for technicians), and to the 'Hauptschule' (the lowest level schools, mostly attended by immigrants from poor families), met with extreme resistance. The basically instinctive fear of the rich and educated families to send their children to schools where they have to mix with those coming from lower social classes put up a fierce opposition to such a reform, and prevented attempts to do away with an elitist and archaic educational system. From my exchanges with people of non-German-speaking countries I believe that the attempt to introduce such a system elsewhere would be branded as 'racist', and would have no chance to be implemented or even considered. It is however deeply engraved in German society's mindset, and is almost taken for a normal feature of a natural selection process. Interestingly enough it turns out that, if a society doesn't open itself, historic circumstances will force it to do so. After the turmoil and wars in the

Middle-East and Afghanistan, millions of immigrants flooded the European continent, especially Germany, and consequently schools were compelled to embrace a stream of immigrant children they can no longer refuse and ignore.

Another example, more mundane, but nicely modern, of the 'what if' fear instinct seems to have occurred with Google's '20% time' rule, which was an intuitive (probably unconscious) understanding of the human being's personal inner potential. The famous search engine company once encouraged its engineers to take 20 percent of their time to indulge their passions for independent projects (needless to say that an FPH or FPU will apply the 100% rule). Indeed several Google products were born in this way (e.g. Gmail and Google News). But subsequently Google abandoned this practice since its managers, once the company and its projects grew larger, feared that this rule could hamper the productivity of the established projects.

Another argument against the FPE concept assumes that it is good only for seers and artists, but not for engineers working in an industry, or for managers. According to Tony Wagner, an Innovation Education Fellow at the Technology & Entrepreneurship Center at Harvard, there are seven survival skills as defined by business leaders in their own words (91): critical thinking and problem solving, collaboration across networks and leading by influence, agility and adaptability, initiative and entrepreneurship, effective oral and written communication, accessing and analysing information, and curiosity and imagination. Each of these can be addressed easily in a free-progress perspective considering that present-day institutions (indirectly or even directly influenced by the business world), while advocating them, however, do not allow these skills to develop individually and to grow freely. If problems are imposed without the allowance for individual question solving, it is then quite obvious that students lack of critical thinking. And how can you learn to lead by influence, and not by authority, if the environment you are growing up in is essentially an authoritarian system? Moreover, it is useless to call for adaptability to change when the schools the students have attended themselves obey a moribund authority's order without questioning it. How can someone who has never, or scarcely ever, been allowed to take initiatives at his/her own risk and responsibility suddenly become a self-directed and creative individual? Where should passionate communication skills come from when all passion was killed long ago by the very same people who now ask for it? How can information processing become effective when you have been raised in a place where it has always been pre-processed for you? No wonder that a research and book by Richard

Arum and Josipa Roksa, (92) which used survey responses and standardized assessment measures, reveals that 45% of students attending higher education institutions in the US don't learn anything in their first two years, and demonstrate no significant improvement in a range of skills such as critical thinking and complex reasoning. And it is no wonder either that Arum and Roksa were criticized for their understanding of what 'learning' means. This was only to be expected in a society that has slowly but steadily begun to understand that the 'reductio ad numerum' of human cognitive activity is untenable. Finally, as to the seventh point, that on curiosity and imagination, it explains itself.

It might be useful in this regard to recall why some giant global corporations became quickly, despite their almost monopolistic position on the world market, insignificant players or even fell into bankruptcy when they had to confront disruptive innovations. An interesting case study is the Eastman Kodak Corporation, commonly known as Kodak. Kodak was the world's largest camera film manufacturer for almost all of its existence, but became utterly unable to reinvent itself when digital photography appeared on the scene, and finally went bankrupt in 2012. The common belief is that Kodak did not understand how digital photography would have quickly replaced the classical film photography. But it can't be as simple as that, since Kodak tried desperately to flood the market with its own digital cameras and other digital hardware and software for many years and, by the way, was the inventor of digital photography itself! Yet, it failed. Most of the financial analysis on this case stops at the superficial conclusion that Kodak did not catch up with a culture of technology innovation and change. What plagued Kodak in its last two decades was poor strategic decisions which tried to launch products doomed to failure. But, after all, this does not explain the root causes why it missed the opportunity of the digital age. While the world was changing due to the digital revolution, in a century-old high-tech company that had thousands of employees, suddenly no one had any longer some good idea to come up with it? That's hard to believe. As John Kotter, Professor Emeritus at Harvard Business School, puts it, the decisive question is: Why did Kodak make the poor strategic decisions they made? At a closer inspection it becomes clear now that *"the organization overflowed with complacency". "Of course all the people buried in the hierarchy who saw the oncoming problems and had ideas for solutions made no progress. Their bosses and peers ignored them"*. (93) Kodak's collapse is at its core a classic example of the inescapable deficiency inherent in a top-down hierarchy model which ignores its own human capital: it was the unwillingness of the CEO and the few leaders at the top of the pyramid to listen to its base that turned out to be the fatal shot. I'm no expert in business and corporate management, but it is difficult to escape the impression that similar reasons might have played a decisive role also in many other giant corporations such as, just to mention some recent cases, the downfall of AT&T, Nokia or Motorola. And this might explain somewhat IBM's and HP's initial reluctance to use its IT know-how in order to catch up with the emerging PC-based technology of the late 1970s.

Therefore, there are good reasons to believe that an FPE is not just for eccentric humanists who crave more freedoms, but it might well prepare future business leaders even much better than any traditional institution which tries to force skills into young brains with mechanical compulsion and a hierarchical mindset.

Anyhow, facts have shown that it is very unlikely that change will come from within the present system. Those who made it through the hierarchy, no matter how much they complain privately, are forced to remain institutionally conservative. Because most are quite comfortable with their actual position and tend not to support fundamental reforms out of fear and incertitude about the future: what comes after might be even worse. The present school and university system is rotten to the core. The hope that more money, more staff, more hardware, and more reforms will make things different is only a self-induced delusion that tries to hide the fear of real change.

Only completely new alternative learning-centres, funded and governed independently of the existing system, will have a chance to do so. The final aim/vision/ideal would be that of an independent school and university campus, where students are free to grow inwardly by liberating their inner soul and higher mind which manifest in a natural talent and an inner power that expresses itself in research, learning, inquiring, a place that has no financial ties or political and bureaucratic connections to present institutions and where students can learn what they want, can do research in the way they feel.

What a Free-Progress-School & University might look like

"We are going to have to find ways of organizing ourselves cooperatively, sanely, scientifically, harmonically, and in regenerative spontaneity with the rest of humanity around the earth .... We are not going to be able to operate our spaceship earth successfully nor for much longer unless we see it as a whole spaceship and our fate as common. It has to be everybody or nobody." - R.
Buckminster Fuller (94)

The question at this point is: what can be done now as a first step towards this vision? After my disappointing personal experiences in several study and working environments, a vision came into being: something which conceives of a learning centre not only for primary and secondary education but also at higher education levels, and which gives people the possibility to express themselves, practise self-learning, and grow by means of an intellectual and intuitive learning process that the standard educational paradigm does not consider, and even openly discourages. A place where students can freely navigate their path to knowledge, and study what their inner being suggests in complete autonomy, not what the faculty imposes. A place where all can pursue their own research lines, and even exercise intuitive approaches that are strictly forbidden in today's institutions.

What follows is only a raw draft, a sketch I tried to lay down for a new educational paradigm. Time will certainly show its drawbacks, and the paradigm may have to undergo change by trial and error as circumstances demand, since there is no real example which is at present in existence and could be taken as a reference. But what is clear is that one of the mistakes committed in the past, for example by the Waldorf pedagogical approach, was to set some principles once and for all, and treat them as eternal truths. These models were indeed new and revolutionary at their times. But an attitude that does not allow for a further evolutionary development, and especially for criticism of the original ideas of their founders, makes them outdated doctrines that no longer fit the needs of modern times. Therefore, while I believe the time has come to set new principles and new organizational, pedagogical, and didactical structures, it is of paramount importance to consider these only as provisional. Everything written in this document must be taken as only a temporary understanding and ideal, which must be continuously subjected to critical assessment and a dynamic change. I would not be surprised to discover that when I reread this document in the future, I will probably even disagree with myself in regard to several aspects. The ideals and principles of an FPE must be regularly revised, changed, and adapted to the present situations. They must be in a continuous transformation at any moment, like a flexible and living organism, and be able to remould themselves like the phoenix of legend. Principles, rules, laws, constitutions, or any written document that regulates the life and work in a free progress system, must always lend themselves to re-examination and revision at regular intervals. This proviso is vital so that what is now considered a new and revolutionary ideal may not return to being an old, encrusted paradigm, resistant to change.

The pedagogical foundations for a
Free-Progress-School and University

Having said that, however, we must begin from where we are and what we have. Some ideas, concepts of organizations, principles, and structural outlines must be set down in black and white. The time has come for us to take the risk of change, without fear of the future, to expose what is no longer tolerable, to detach ourselves from the present system and yoke of power, and to criticize and complain, and, at the same time, to propose realistic and practical alternative ways to proceed. While outlining the structural and administrative foundations of an FPH and FPU, we have to keep in mind some core ideas which may serve as indicators for the new pedagogy. A free-progress environment is not a lawless freedom, chaos, or just a place where we may do whatever we want without regard for others' rights. Quite the contrary, there might be even more rules and even forms of reprimand. But the rules imposed must have a twofold complementary function: guarantee not only the collective quality of the school or university, but also the individual freedom of expression as long as it does not hurt others.

Let us begin with the traditional idea of the teacher or professor. It is that of an authority that has competence in a specific subject, and whose main responsibility is to transfer this knowledge from his/her own brain into other brains (with more or less authoritarian methods and threatening means like exams and grades). In the new educational paradigm the student alone is responsible for his/her self-education. The choice of the subject to study and of the learning methods are completely left to the student. What has to be learned must be determined from a desire to learn, a curiosity to know, from an inner authority. There is no longer someone who 'teaches', but only a learning mentor who suggests (and only when asked for a suggestion), helps if asked, eventually lectures, but only to arouse curiosity, spirit of inquiry, and nobody should resort to a blind repetition of his syllabus. Because lecturing provides data and information and, eventually, some training. However, training is not real learning that leads to knowledge, understanding and wisdom, which are kept so accurately out of the equation. The ideal school and university is that in which there is no teaching, eventually some training, best replaced by self-training methodologies, but a lot of learning. The main purpose of the new system is to guide the student to self-discovery. The professionalism and preparation of a learning mentor will be judged from the pedagogical skills and the understanding of the essence and the motivation that the learner experiences, not for the intellectual knowledge of a subject, which should become secondary. The hiring of learning mentors should be proposed by students.

In a conventional school setting children are strictly organized into classes and grades according to their age. Does this age-wise grouping in classrooms make sense? Of course, a six years old child cannot learn calculus or quantum mechanics as a graduate student, and an 18-year-old high school student who is preparing for graduation won't spent time in studying with a primary school child. However, my experience as a teacher showed me clearly how this strict compartmentalization in fine-grained age groups is not only artificial and unnatural but also harmful to the psychological and intellectual development of all those who do not fit precisely into the supposed maturity and developmental stage they are expected to be at their age. As every teacher knows all too well, in every class there are pupils who are already several grades further ahead in their cognitive and emotional maturity than others, while there are likely to be some who are behind. Both suffer, since the former are not allowed to develop their innate skills and their potential is suppressed, while the latter are forced to do and learn stuff they are still not mature enough to manage. Only a minority find themselves at the right place at the right moment.

A pedagogical and didactical dynamic that rests on the idea that our mental and psychological development can be described from childhood to adulthood in a tight and strict temporal order is flawed from the outset, simply because experience contradicts it. In an FPE environment this idea of classes organized into grades must be given up completely. Children should eventually group themselves naturally in age groups if they feel so, but should not be forced to do so. If a six-year-old can master the maths of a third-grade child, they should learn together despite their difference in age. If a boy of 16 likes to play football with an eight-year-old child, there should be no objection from the adults side. And if the older students themselves like to help younger ones by teaching them what they have already learned, why separate them into boxes which prevent them from interacting? In an free-progress-school (FPS), FPH or FPU environment age will no longer be an exclusive parameter which is supposed to determine the place and learning path of a child or student. All will group and re-group themselves naturally whenever and however they wish. Forcibly graded classrooms will no longer exist.

But what about the reasons for pursuing a study? We are accustomed to think of education as a learning practice that should prepare us for a professional life and for making a living. But the main aim of FPE is the liberation of the inner spirit, the finding of our own direction, the freedom to be intellectually and spiritually what we really are. Career and financial perspectives must be subordinate necessities, not the decisive factor. The dictatorship of time and deadlines must fall. It takes time to let flourish intuition, insight, and wisdom. Where is the time for contemplation? Those who are marathoners that learn slowly, but might become able to delve more deeply into a subject, should not be pressured as if they are sprinters. Sprinters also should be free to finish their studies earlier than the official academic rules have set for their academic path, if they feel so.

The standard learning paradigm is focused on an analytic understanding. Here, in the new system, the learning process does not focus as much on acquiring knowledge as on competence. There is a subtle difference between knowledge and know-how. We do not need to become a mobile encyclopaedia, with mountains of facts pressed into our brain, but to cultivate technical, as well as social skills and competences. While the rational approach should continue to maintain its place as a tool of knowledge in every human activity, it should at the same time not be detrimental to other forms of gnosis. Great intellectual achievements have frequently as their basis inspirations coming from a contemplative dimension. The dreamer, the seer, the visionary, the really independent thinker is not necessarily always guided by a strictly logical theory made of inferences and deductions. Modern-day schools, and universities, pay almost no attention to the inner subjective nature of the mind and the heart. Schools and universities should open themselves up to contemplative and intuitional methods which foster inspirations and revelations (e.g. by self-mastering the mind and body with meditation techniques, mindfulness, or complementary approaches like Goethian science). Some attempts that go in this direction have already been made for example by scientists like Arthur Zajonc, director of the Center for Contemplative Mind in Society (52). In this view we can enhance our learning skills through mindfulness, contemplative teaching and learning, cognitively oriented spirituality (self-control, attention, concentration, meditation), focusing with attention exercises, strengthening and cultivating mental and emotional capacities, by learning to pay attention to the present moment non-judgementally and by a de-automatization of our habitual tendencies, etc. (95)

In our present culture, 'learning' is associated with a measurable acquisition of notions, facts, and skills, possibly without failures, which the student must be able to reproduce. The direct experience as such with all its mental, emotional, and physical content is not considered learning, as long as it doesn't produce tangible results in the form of new intellectual insights that answer precise questions. At best, it is perceived as an enriching, playful activity, just a game, but not as a possible learning experience. Only the result of a successful experiment or investigation which produces knowledge that can be translated into a set of analytic concepts, possibly with potential outcomes useful for a future career, is considered real 'learning'. This is a deep-rooted idea in our culture and mentality. And yet history as well as cognitive sciences tell us that most of the skills are acquired at stages of activity where failure, doubts, and unanswered questions are still predominant. The doing in itself, as such, conceivably without results, or even with failures, is a learning process, too. This means that, unlike in didactical approaches of the past, learning in an FPS, FPH and FPU environment does not occur by imitation (typically, by repeating the lecture or solving preordered exercises), but it does by an exercise of one's own skills. No preconceived programmes or timetables dictate the content and pace of the learning process. The student alone must know, feel, and perceive inwardly, and therefore be left totally free to act in this regard (theory vs. experiment, focusing on one or another approach or procedure, choosing different textbooks than those suggested by the learning mentor, taking the short or long path, etc.).

Any form of learning or academic research should not be judged or evaluated by its practical potential. Present academia inoculates some skills which are supposed to be useful for your future job which the state or community will (hopefully) offer. In a free-progress environment, the philosopher who asks about the essence of the world should not have any less freedom to express an inner thirst for pure knowledge than is available to the pragmatist interested in developing a new piece of hardware for industry and the market. Studying, learning, and doing research should no longer be tied to their potential to produce material wealth, or to the actuality of the current research trend or paradigm. Again, it is the student's or researcher's choice of direction in which to move, and no committee of sages or higher hierarchies should have any say in the matter.

Education should prepare us first of all to discover and develop our inherent skills, independently of their potential for practical applications.

Several pedagogues have wondered whether it is the weaknesses of children that it is sensible to focus on, or their strengths. The former approach rests on the standard assumption that everyone has to learn the same basic concepts, and all must acquire a set of fundamental notions. The latter assumes that each of us has some strengths, not just because of a coincidence, but because every soul has an existential programme that serves the development of the individual, as well as that of the community. This existential programme encodes the strengths which should be used to manifest our life mission. The weaknesses are not a capricious joke of nature, but could well be less developed skills which are less necessary for the unfoldment of the particular individual, and it would be therefore a waste of time and energy to concentrate on the weaknesses. In the new educational paradigms, the emphasis is set on cultivating the strengths, and a learning mentor should primarily encourage the further development of these instead of forcing upon the learner skills which are not his or hers. However, on the other side, sometimes weaknesses are also the sign of undeveloped or wrongly developed nature of the being due to past wrong choices or bad habits or experiences. There is no dilemma here. The solution is, as usual, in freedom. It should be left to the free choice of the student eventually to focus attention on the weak aspects of the personal character. But this choice should come from within, not from a source forced, superimposed, and ordered by someone who may not know the real inner causes of these weaknesses.

Today schools, and even more so do universities, measure the skills of their students with a few parameters: the amount of information encapsulated by the brain, the time needed to reproduce a task based on that information (typically there is a strict time limit to solve an exercise, while an oral examination needs an immediate feedback), and the number of correct answers finally determine the grade awarded. But this implies that what is measured is what we know, not what we can do or can know. The insight, intuitive understanding, and the result of a passionate study which needs more time and an inner perception of the work to be done, are considered inessential. In the context of FPE, where exams and grades are abolished, these superficial evaluations play a secondary role. Of course students have to take their responsibilities. The (self-)assigned task has to be completed in reasonable time, the quality of the work done could be reviewed by a commission (which includes students and eventually some forms of evaluations, but without grades), codes of behaviour must be respected, and so forth.

The time factor is of central value here. Great discoveries have sometime been made quickly, paradoxically just because the discoverer was not under time pressure. Our brain sometimes needs incubation times to find the right answer. It does not work as in textbook problem solving. It works according to a path and pace where, sometimes also long times of incubation, evolution, and maturation, apparently without tangible outer results, are needed, and that must be allowed before, sometimes suddenly, it reaches the heights of a new and original idea.

Summing up, what follows is a list of proposed actions to be taken for FPE in comparison with the ordinary education paradigm.

Ordinary education	Free-Progress-Education
Top-down teaching: the teacher/professor tells class what should be learned. Motivation is fostered, if at all, by extrinsic means. The student receives teaching.	Bottom-up learning: the learning mentor helps the student to discover what his/her inner being wants to learn. Intrinsic motivation has precedence over the extrinsic one. The student practises self-directed-teaching methods.
The choice and quality of the content to be taught has paramount importance.	The quality of the learning mentor is much more important.
The aim is to become fit in being competitive in the modern world and in the choice of a career.	The aim is to discover what your purpose in this life is, give it a meaning, the means to pursue it, through a 'learning to learn' process. Cooperation is favoured over competition.
Children are distributed in grades and classrooms according to an age-wise grouped scheme.	All pupils and students play and learn together without distinction of age. There are study rooms but no system of age-wise structured classrooms.
The school sets fixed learning schedules.	Allow for incubation times. Everyone has his own time of growth!

Analytic-rational exercise.	Contemplative approach.
Learn by imitating what has been done. The institution sets the goal.	Learn by doing what your inner call suggests. The student selects the goal.
Everything is focused on acquiring knowledge aiming at production.	Focus on understanding and doing following your own call. It is not so much about knowledge but competences.
Works on the weaknesses. A lot of emphasis is set on acquiring so called 'basic concepts'.	Works on the strengths. Who decides what is 'basic'? There is something in us that knows much better than anyone else what basic knowledge is good for us.
Fostering skills, speed, and efficiency in reproducing specific tasks.	Fostering interest, curiosity, talent, and inclinations.

The structural foundations for a Free-Progress-School and University

In the following pages we would like to name those aspects that should be abolished entirely from the modern educational machinery and what instead could be alternatively introduced.

First of all, the elimination of exams from a new school, college and university educational system is of paramount importance. Exams have always been a means of submission, fear, and even political power, inside a command and control system, not a tool which fosters real learning. Real learning is not made of a repetition of concepts regurgitated in an academic course. Real learning can only happen in a self-directed and self-controlled system, through self-acquirement of notions, the deeper understanding through direct experience, the unfoldment of the spirit in learning, instead of the repression of creativity by reiterating a litany to an instructor who looks at the student from above, and menaces retaliation with a bad grade. The compulsion with grading has its roots in the obsession for an enumerative knowledge where everything must be standardized and quantified. Because of this obsession for standardization according to which 'one size should fit all' and the quantitative assessment of things, we have lost our innate ability not only to appreciate the qualitative aspects of the individual, but also our ability to see the strengths of people. In some sense, we might say that in schools and universities there has never been real learning. It is this mentality which led to the US 'No Child Left Behind' program first and the government centralized standardized tests conceptions of 'Common Core Standards' laws in education later, and which are now under severe criticism.

Moreover, grading inhibits the trial-and-error method which is extremely important in a process of discovery. Grading enhances the fear of failure, while failure itself should be honoured as the master in learning. Churchill used to say, *'Success consists of going from failure to failure without loss of enthusiasm.'* There is no scientific evidence that correlates grades of students with the skills, the efficiency, and their performance at the future working place. So, what are grades useful for, after all? They are only useful for the system which prefers quantitative standardization, since it is the easiest way to sort out people, but certainly not according to a quality criterion. Grades are mere etiquettes which represent the most extreme form of reductionism since they are supposed to describe what we know and what we can (and finally, also what we are) in a few numbers or letters. The best knowledge and best skills are not imposed but are self-acquired through a passionate, fearless learning operation by doing things while following one's own inner need for knowledge and curiosity. It is about learning and doing research as long as the student or researcher discovers where the strengths are, and once found, go for it! Grading is a form of a not-so-subtle degradation. Grading and fostering passion, creativity, initiative, and curiosity are mutually exclusive. There is no objective way to quantify the intrinsic nature of these values. That is why, despite every effort to the contrary, they remain inevitably expunged from all those systems which maintain standardized quantitative evaluations. Grade-based institutions that claim to foster intrinsic motivation are deluding themselves.

In the present educational systems, students pay for a degree, not for an education. They are so focused on acquiring the degree, possibly with high grades, that there is virtually no time left to follow their own innate interests. What we need is not reforms of the actual primitive examinations and grading and degree systems, but an abolishment of the system itself. Under FPE, there won't be exams, grades, and certificates, but a regulated system which certifies that a student has attended the school for a specific length of time, and produced some research or intellectual work of their own.

In this view, a possible alternative to certificates could be the 'development portfolio': the student's achievements could be documented by creating a 'learning biography', in the form of a thesis, dissertation, publications of peer-reviewed papers, a book, the realization of experiments in a laboratory, creating and managing their own learning experiences producing interactive material that is available online to everyone (so called 'open source learning' (96)) or any other product or creative presentation that documents the work done, the project developed and the results achieved. This could be presented to a selected panel of experts appointed by the general assembly (see next section), in order to prove the skills and abilities that the student acquired during his/her attendance at the FPH or FPU. The portfolio is therefore an education map that documents the performance in the form of an internship report, and that represents an individual's education path and the skills acquired. The important point here is the principle of complete assumption of responsibility. No learning mentor must take responsibility for the work done, and, apart from eventual acknowledgments or personal appreciations, should not appear in a report, thesis, dissertation, etc. as a 'tutor'. The FPH and FPU must also explicitly disclaim any direct and indirect responsibility for the quality and accuracy of the work. The work accomplished represents only and exclusively the student's good or bad performance.

Another aspect that vitiates present schools and academia is admission requirements. We always tend to elaborate an analytic formula or imagine a concept which (usually in a quantitative manner) tries to assess who is 'admissible', and who is not. Again, tests and grades are worked out and these are supposed to determine who is the 'right one' for attending the courses, and who is not. But the truth is that there is no such selection rule that is able to measure skills which result from an inner fire for perfection and aspiration for knowledge and action. All these selection criteria have all too often been shown to obtain a result just the opposite of what they were designed for: the de-selection of many who later turned out to be the most gifted ones, but were not recognized by a society which itself did not live up to the call of its time.

In the standard financial college and university paradigms students have to pay huge fees in order to be allowed to attend, being drilled, submit themselves to an authoritarian and stressful academic path, with the aim to obtain finally that piece of paper, a certificate. In a free-progress learning community, fees must be kept as low as possible, ideally there should be none, and the aim is not a certificate but self-development on a self-directed learning base.

Also references in the form of letters of presentation should be banned altogether. The point is that these are a means of perpetuation of the system. Not the best students, but the most servile and adapted ones, are those that obtain references from their tutor. Those who have developed a more critical sense, and might not be docile workers who please the hierarchy and might be less skilled in political games, eventually possessing also a shy and reserved character, will find themselves more isolated, and it will become difficult to find teachers or professors willing to write something in their favour. This is an absurd practice that is only useful for moulding obedient servants, not independent thinkers. Therefore, there should be no need for references or letters of presentation. In case where the number of students must be limited exclusively because of logistic or financial reasons, then the 'first come, first served' rule should be applied. It should be as simple as that.

Then we have to entirely reconsider the relationship between the teacher or professor to the student. The idea of an adult that is at the top of a pyramidal hierarchy that knows better what is good or bad for a young learner must finally be abandoned. Nothing can be taught really. One can only guide or help someone else to find the truth and knowledge by and in himself/herself. Learning must no longer be a systemized machinery of notions and stuff imparted by someone who supposedly knows, but an activity which arises by a free choice of the students who will teach themselves. Teachers and professors must learn to forget their old, outdated role, and become learning mentors who follow students in their learning path, and do so only if they are expressly requested by the student. Learning mentors should take advantage of the possibility to learn themselves. They should learn too by their activity, and accept also that the roles might be exchanged: the student can equally well teach the learning mentor. Everyone should be allowed to become a learning mentor, for example, by proposing a course, even first-year students, if they feel they have had sufficient preparation and skills. The basic idea should be that once new knowledge and skills are learned, they should be transmitted as soon as possible, for example, by exercising the LdL method, without having to wait until promotions and academic titles materialize. The strict division based on an authority who knows and has power over a class of students that must absorb some mental stuff, has to be abolished once and for all. Learning mentors could be hired either by the school or department, or by the students themselves who should be allowed to subject their candidacy to the general assembly.

About curricula, the following might be said. There are essentially two schools of thought about the subject. The first one, i.e. the traditional point of view, is that there is a basic body of knowledge that everyone should and must learn, willingly or not, because (this is the belief) the inexpert mind of a novice student can't know what really should have priority. For example, in physics, every student without exception is supposed to learn about the principles of mechanics, thermodynamics, electromagnetism, and so forth. The opposite point of view affirms that this is nowadays an anachronistic model of teaching since, due to the explosion of disciplines and discoveries over the past centuries, the so-called general knowledge is no longer possible, and, at any rate, if someone wants to acquire an intellectual expertise in some subject, in the form of a sterile information and data set, the Internet is such a powerful knowledge tool that nobody really needs to follow a preordered academic curriculum. In FPE, this apparent dilemma is reconciled again taking the freedom of the soul as the guiding principle. There should be the freedom of the learning mentor to express some line of thought and content organizing it in a more or less articulate syllabus and course structure, but on the other hand there should be also the freedom of the student to accept it, or reject it partially or entirely, turning his/her attention in other directions if the class isn't considered satisfying or interesting enough. This saves both perspectives, a school can offer a wholly comprehensive academic path, yet everyone is free to choose the parts according to personal preferences, modify it or propose an entirely different one.

In the free-progress system, there are no admission rules for students at all. However, due to technical or financial reasons, a selection and admission of some sort might nevertheless be necessary in the case of learning mentors and the technical and administrative staff responsible for the didactical and technical maintenance of the school or university who may be required to show their ability and preparation. Modern schools and societies, advanced in the recognition of human rights, have realized the importance of preventing sex, race, physical, and age discrimination. However, the fact remains that it is considered completely par for the course to ask for gender, ethnic origin, age, or disability in an application form for admission to a school or college, or even for a grant or a position at these institutions. This opens the doors not only to a willed and controlled discrimination during a selection phase, but, even if such information is used for proper purposes as it is supposed to be, it still can influence a commission that has to judge one's skills. Of course, during an interview the physical aspects can hardly be concealed, but a free-progress selection commission should do its utmost to disclose them as late as possible during the selection process (for example, by asking for only CVs without photographs and personal data of the candidate). Research proposals should be as blind as possible with the evaluating committee having no information on the applicant's background or publishing record.

All this can be summarized with the following set of proposals which elucidate what new forms of teaching and learning could be introduced in a free-progress educational institution.

Abolition of	Proposal
Exams	Effectuation of a system that fosters/guides free knowledge and self-directed learning. Free choice of performance in front of the community.
Grades	Non-quantitative judgement but qualitative advice by learning mentors and students on how to proceed.
Degrees	Development portfolio: certification of attendance and productivity, only with qualitative, non-quantitative assessment, if necessary
Admission requirements	Everyone is allowed to participate.
Huge tuition fees for being allowed to submit oneself to a 'via crucis' with the prospect of a degree	No fees or admission costs, or as low as possible. The FPS, FPH or FPU student does not pay for a degree but, if at all, for a chance of self-development.
References	An advisor who needs second-

	hand judgement and isn't able to recognize the skills of a student should quit the job.
Traditional student-teacher-professor pyramidal hierarchies	No hierarchies of 'teachers' or 'professors' exist. Only learning mentors and students that eventually even exchange their roles by exchanging knowledge.
Curriculum and syllabus	Learning mentors' freedom to structure any kind of syllabus they desire. Student's freedom to refuse it and re-structure it accordingly to his/her own skills.
Race, gender, age, or physical criteria	If selection rules must be applied, then, as far as possible, without age, gender, personal data, or handicap disclosure. In case of research proposal, without publishing and career records.

The didactical foundations for a Free-Progress-School and University

As to the learning methods, a variety of different approaches have emerged in the last years which suggest new ways of learning and they could perhaps become the backbone of a new FPS, FPH and FPU.

The material concept should provide state-of-the-art educational technology forming a networked community, based on an open-source ideal, and with free access to MOOCs which will enable students to learn also from professors and courses at any outside university in the world.

MOOCs are a relatively recent development in distance education, and their effectiveness remains to be seen. But it is hard to believe that new technologies might not, in one way or another, play a role and become a fundamental infrastructure of new learning paradigms. What is important is not just the technical capabilities of the new technologies, but their usefulness in the pedagogical and didactical approach that we are advocating. The professor-centred open online courses known as xMOOCs, are a format that still prevails because it reflects the traditional lecturer-to-scholar approach. But other forms of online learning with interactive engagements might well change this with time. For example, a department may entirely abolish the traditional format of courses held by a professor. The university may select the best online courses available on the Internet worldwide, and collect them together in a program which will furnish the same skills and know-how that a conventional diploma, bachelor, masters, or Ph.D. delivers. Each course could have its set of online lectures. The online lectures can be discussed, with exercises solved in the classroom collectively with the help of the learning mentor physically present. The learning mentor's main function would therefore not be to deliver content, but to help the students to assimilate and discuss offline what was previously taught online (and eventually complement it with his/her own content). The assimilation could also express itself with other online courses created by the students themselves, in the form of a y-MOOC (you-MOOC). A y-MOOC distinguishes itself from the x-MOOC in that it is not created by a renewed academic authority that has been authorized by a university, but nevertheless may present new knowledge, understandings, or didactical and pedagogical approaches that were previously not known or considered. Everyone of us has some expertise to share with the world, even though that might not imply the possession of a degree or hierarchical position in the system.

'**Blended learning**' mixes traditional classroom activities mediated by technology (student with a tablet or laptop, or small groups working together on devices). Students learn in part through online delivery while still attending a brick-and-mortar school.

'**Peer instruction**' is a method which replaces lectures with small group discussions of conceptual questions, followed by whole-class discussions, with mini-lectures between questions. Students first think about the problem and answer these questions individually; then discuss the explanations for their answers with their neighbours and come to agreement.

'**Flip teaching**' (or 'flipped classroom') is a form of blended learning in which students learn first from video lectures, and do in class what used to be homework (assigned problems), with learning mentors offering more personalized guidance and interaction instead of lecturing.

The 'SOLE method' of Sugata Mitra is based on several forms of blended learning and flip teaching in a DIY U style. It encourages dynamic interaction among students to work as a community in groups in order to answer assigned questions or even self-posed questions through online material or otherwise. Again, while it was conceived only for children, there is no reason to believe that it cannot be applied to adults too.

Lais natural learning inspired by a Schetinin School style learning method and the Lais natural learning movement, whereby pupils learn from one another in groups, without teacher-centred teaching. The paradigm focuses on our innate way to learn through direct experience by trial and error. Following their own interests and mutual learning experiences which allow space for errors the child learns faster and develops many more skills compared to the standard 'chalk and talk' teaching methods.

The 'learning by teaching' (LdL) method of Jean-Pol Martin, which relies on the idea of promoting students to teachers. The students prepare the lesson at home, and later explain it to their classmates. Through an active style of networked participation and discussion, each student asks questions, or proposes new solutions. The function of the 'real' teacher, i.e. the learning mentor, becomes one of support to the process, but remains in the background.

Inquiry Based Learning (IBL) is an outgrowth and generalization of the 'Moore Method', a learning technique introduced in the mid-20th century by R. L. Moore, an American mathematician and a part of a more general Problem Based Learning (PBL) method. According to the Centre for Inquiry-Based Learning of the University of Sheffield, `IBL´ describes a cluster of strongly student-centred approaches to learning and teaching that are driven by inquiry or research. Students conduct small or large-scale inquiries that enable them to engage actively with the concepts and questions of their discipline, often in collaboration with each other. Learning takes place through an emergent process of exploration and discovery. Guided by subject specialists and those with specialist roles in learning support, students use the scholarly and research practices of their disciplines to move towards autonomy in creating and sharing knowledge. (97)

The 'barcamp' or 'un-conference' modality might play a role in a future higher education environment also. A barcamp might be defined as an alternative way with which people could communicate their ideas, projects, studies, and even dreams. It works as follows. In the beginning, all the people convene in a hall, and everyone is allowed to present in a minute or two his or her session. And 'everyone' means just that: everyone. There is no hierarchy of sages, teachers, or professors. Also a perfectly unknown person could rush in and present a speech. 'Mister nobody' can propose for instance to discuss with those who like to attend 'the future of MOOCs', or instead of presenting his own project he might ask for solutions to questions such as how to find funds to publish a book on hand surgery, or discuss how far didactical and pedagogical optimism is justified, and so on. Once the session has been briefly presented, and if among those present some raise their hands to show interest, a room and a time segment for a discussion are assigned. The same procedure repeats itself for all the others who present a topic. In this fashion, several sessions will have been programmed, without any previous intervention or approval by a commission. On a board, in less than a half an hour, a huge programme of sessions is set. Then everyone attends those which are considered the most interesting. What follows is not a talk by the proponent of the session, but only a brief introduction, after which an informal discussion is opened to all those present. The idea is that the classical seminar format might be occasionally replaced also by 'un-seminars'. This doesn't necessarily mean that the traditional seminar is going to die. However, in several situations a barcamp-style seminar might be a better solution because seminars are used to convey information. Instead, an un-seminar can function as a platform to ask for information. For example, one might have an idea for a research project, and might want to hear what other students and faculty members might think of it. Another might want to set up a research group, and to look for members wishing to join in. Yet another might wish to share opinions and impressions about a new discovery, and so on. The barcamp, un-conference, and un-seminar formats might prove to be a great tool for communicating among students and university members ideas, projects, findings, news, etc. That would also foster a real socialization and new forms of group work, which are not forced and imposed from above, as they are at the present time.

'Open Space meetings' are a new and simple approach to run meetings with a few or many people, and a way to organize the exchange of experiences, knowledge, and information in everyday practice in a continuously changing environment. The goal is to create inspiring meetings where people work together on a regular basis to create some result or work together towards some common aim. The difference from the standard form of meeting is that in an Open Space meeting participants create and manage parallel working sessions which focus on different aspects of a common theme. This approach has a more active connotation for the participants, each having a great passion but a different perspective on a subject. Participants arrange themselves in a circle and start with no prior agenda, which is set by the group at the beginning of the session. Each individual presents a topic, raises issues, makes comments, asks questions, and so on. A further advantage is that all participants feel engaged in the process, and that everyone's ideas, proposals, or doubts are acknowledged and eventually discussed by the entire group. It produces a dynamic exchange of ideas and creates an atmosphere of commonness in the elaboration of new ideas and assimilation of the issues and questions, in a dynamic, problem-solving approach. Open Space could be especially useful in high schools and universities which are at present too much centred on the individual learning of the 'lonely student scheme'. It could be used to pave the way to more sophisticated forms of cooperation.

'Spontaneous co-creative cooperation' vs. traditional teamwork should replace the conventional group-think and teamwork philosophies. Almost everyone would agree that young generations should learn more to engage in a collective activity and become fit for teamwork. Being able to socialize, and to cultivate a team spirit in order to be part of a working group striving for a common goal, is continuously spoken of as a critical and compelling skill future societies will need. It is therefore puzzling to hear expressions of dissatisfaction from many teachers, professors, and managers at the lack of real progress in this regard. It is common to find that many students and workers perceive schools, universities, research centres, and industrial establishments as places where one can only work on the given workload with very weak interaction with colleagues and fellow students. Students are assigned to working groups and asked to collaborate towards a common goal, and frequently different forms of encouragement, united with forms of coercion, are applied to enhance participation and 'esprit de corps'. Almost all companies claim on their websites to value teamwork as a top priority and working method. It has become a fashion, almost a compulsion, to highlight one's dedication to the principle. Nevertheless, despite many efforts, a cohesive team remains an exception, not a rule, and the reality is usually very different than the proclaimed intentions.

The reason for this failure becomes quite clear once we look at it from the 'freedom of the soul' perspective. In fact, it will not be the obsessive preaching and continuous call to teamwork that will bring it to life. The question is not whether teamwork is desirable, the desirability of which is a point on which almost all agree, but how it is to be achieved. This is much less obvious and straightforward. It should be clarified what kind of teamwork we are talking about. A synergic unity of people struggling for a goal is not a modern human activity but as old as humankind itself. It has been extensively applied for thousands of years and meticulously elaborated throughout all cultures and times: in the military. The aim was, and unfortunately still remains, to a large extent even in education, to drill to obedience, conformity, and reverent submission. Of course, no one would ever admit to conceiving of teamwork in these terms. But the truth is probably much more subtle. As the centuries-old educational concepts which reverberate in our minds are unconsciously permeated and moulded by a Winslow Taylor industrial mindset, so is our conception of teamwork which, without having awareness of the underlying cultural influence, relies mainly on a militaristic idea of group efficiency.

For example, despite what we like to believe, in most of present-day research centres, there is no real and true teamwork at all. In a certain sense it is a modern myth. What is called 'teamwork' today is in effect the distribution of tasks inside a larger project area. It is not a real team, but a collection of individuals who are ordered to work together on a common goal. First of all, this serially lining up of working labour is usually forced upon people who could neither choose their work or study collaborators, a situation that frequently leads to a lack of inner psychological accord, nor could they choose the activity they are asked to focus on. Moreover, most times the goal calls for the execution of an enormous set of complex tasks which necessarily assigns to each individual a different one. This leads to an artificial form of teamwork, which is only external, but it is not internalized, because while a whole group of people works to achieve a common goal, rarely do they truly work together on the same task with an inner feeling of being part of a synergic unity. What is even worse, the execution of these tasks is set under pressure of deadlines and strict controls. The result is that everyone works without the freedom to express a real inner potential, conflicts frequently erupt among the members because of the clash of characters, and de facto everyone has to do a job alone (the managerial mindset sometimes deludes itself into believing that this state of affairs can be remedied by calling for permanent and endless group meetings). Conceiving teamwork as a sort of military activity, which aims only at the interests of the collective without taking into account also those of the individual, is only a very limited form of cooperation.

If we look instead at this problem with the lenses of the inner inherent freedom of the human being, it becomes not too difficult to understand where the problem lies. While S. Cain's call (48) for a return to the introvert thinker and the practice of lone thinking must be taken seriously, in a free-progress learning environment, teamwork will remain an essential ingredient of interaction between individuals. True teamwork, integral to the FPE, is a concomitant of educational self-organization. It must rise from a spontaneous congregation of people, each with their own talents and abilities, and not dictated by a director or an authority. Students should be left free to decide with whom to work and study. There should be no fixed a priori task appointed by someone else, but students will have a free choice to pursue the common goal by choosing their own task, as far as possible in friendship with someone else, and remain free to leave when they no longer feel part of the group. Only in such an environment can we begin to speak about real collaboration and spontaneous teamwork.

Spontaneous co-creative cooperation should be based on three basic pillars. First, the freedom to ask the question and/or pose the problem which will lead to the final project proposal. Rarely are students free to learn, investigate, and research for the answers to the questions they have in mind. The exercise, the homework, the knowledge to be achieved are all pre-assigned by the teaching force. Whereas it should be the other way around. Secondly, an individual's freedom to join a group or project according to their own interest or skills, or even to disengage from group work altogether, should be respected. On the other side, members of the group should accept one another. If someone is not desired, the group also should have the power to reject him/her, and those who do not comply with the rules. In conventional schools or academia, the contrary is true: usually students are not free to choose in which group they may work. They are thrown into one or another set of people who are working on something they may not be interested in, and are asked to be collaborative nevertheless. Thirdly, everyone should be free to choose his/her degree of effort in the participation process. This means that everyone can decide how much to be collaborative. The best way to incentivize collaboration is not to force it on the members of a group. In an attempt to foster group dynamics, some professors ask their students even to assess and grade the contribution and group effort of the other members of the group. There are good reasons to believe that this tactic produces even more tension and dissatisfaction.

A spontaneous collaboration must be based on the freedom to ask questions, on the freedom to aggregate and the freedom to participate. This could open the way to a synthesis between team spirit and everyone's own personalized one-on-one mentoring combining it with self-directed experiential learning.

'**Development Portfolio Project based learning**' should become a logical consequence of the above-described learning environment. DPPBL is a model that organizes learning around projects, that is, the inquiry and investigative activities over extended periods of time which could be chosen by students autonomously and culminate in an intellectual, artistic or material accomplishment. In PBL, learning mentors facilitate, but do not direct, and students work usually in groups cooperatively, even though that should not be a necessary condition. The idea of project based learning dates back to J. Dewey (43), but has been adopted and successfully applied in several forms since then. There won't be a certificate-based path in this system, but instead a free (individual or group) tailored research or productive project. The aim is no longer to obtain a certificate, but to acquire knowledge through a self-directed-learning process that will lead to a thesis, a book, articles in peer-reviewed journals or with online open source learning environments, artistic achievements, a hardware product, a new invention, etc. A prospective employer, will not be looking at certificates and grades, which portray a candidate's replication and emulation skills, while not saying much about his/her creative potential. A detailed portfolio of achievements will instead provide a much clearer portrayal of the potential the candidate brings.

The above examples were only some among the many alternative forms of education practiced nowadays worldwide. The list is by no means complete (see many others here (71)). They nevertheless display how many different forms and methods of future learning and teaching are possible. Each of them has a strength of its own, and each might be an appropriate path for some as it may not for others. However, most of them remain isolated cases which did not find further acceptance in the very same institution where they have been applied, since the conservativeness and habitual thought patterns of conventional schools and colleges is much stronger than the experimental spirit of innovation of single groups trying out new forms of learning. Moreover, most of these alternative educational initiatives remained focused on one or the other method but did not even contemplate a conception which attempts to synthesize them into a coherent pedagogical and didactical frame.

In fact, the drawback I see in these methods is that, more or less explicitly, each learning method claims itself separately to be the best for every child or youngster or adult. What they lack is the possibility to choose. For instance, the SOLE and the Lais methods focus excessively on group work and leave aside those who eventually want to learn alone a very specific subject that nobody else is interested in. The LdL might be fine for those who are more extrovert and who like talking in front of an audience but penalizes others who are less skilled in attracting the audience attention and might be nevertheless great learners and be active in some other form. The DPPBL approach is great for those who envisage themselves working onto projects or in research labs, but why not take a good old traditional teacher-centred class?

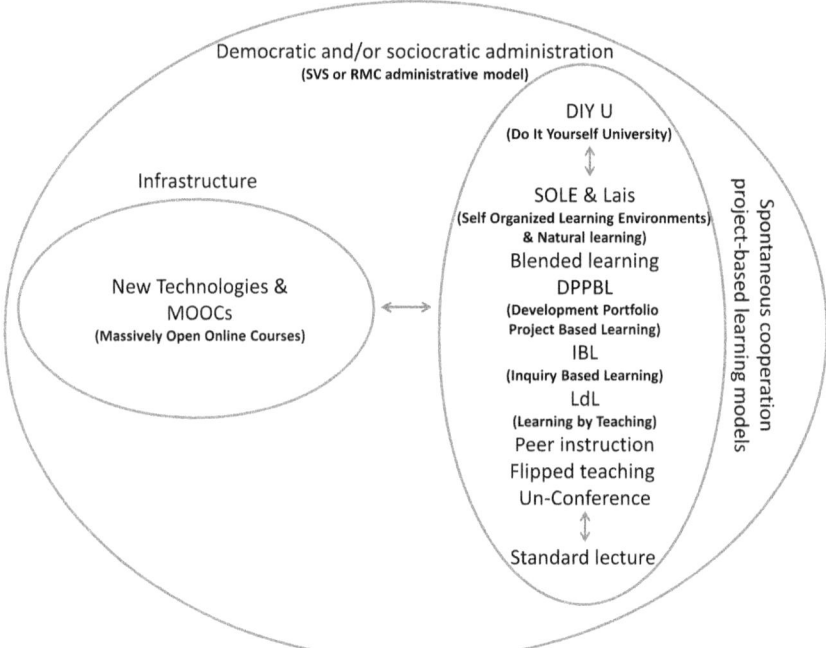

All these approaches still inherit an unconscious compulsory attitude which reverberates the following: "Now we all must learn together according to this new revolutionary education paradigm and you must align yourself to it". Alternatives are again discouraged or banned entirely. One might also a desire to practise for some time one technique and switch later on to another. For example, a student might begin with an auto-didactical approach by reading books or using MOOCs, then participate to a flipped classroom and only later finally set into practice the acquired knowledge and skills by initiating a DPPL. There are infinite possible variations, overlaps and interactions among these different educational pathways. To my likeminded Lais advocates I use to say that real natural learning can not go without self-determined learning. So, choosing the one or the other learning method separately, even if in line with one's own inclinations and preferences, is still not the ideal setup. An element of self-determination is still lacking.

Therefore, to ensure a learning environment based on a passion-driven learning framework, all of these aspects and properties should not taken separately from each other. FPE works as an integrated, interdependent system, a living and learning organism where each one is not only allowed to choose the learning method but has also the freedom to change it with time passing by and according to one's own personal growth. Providing a rich pioneering environment for multiple models of education we could have true freedom to walk out of the system.

The previous diagram tries to summarize some of the aforementioned.

The administrative foundations for a Free-Progress-School and University

The administrative and organizational structure of an FPE setting represents a huge challenge in its direct practical execution. Regulatory norms, codes of behaviour, conflict resolution, and problem-solving approaches must be considered. To the best of the author's knowledge, only some attempts have been made, but so far no existing institution can be said to have the creative self-organizational representative and transparent structure we are trying to outline here. Inevitably, what follows can only be an outline, and must be considered a temporary sketch of ideas. Only actual experience in the real world will show how and where it may have to be amended from time to time.

However, if we were to look for a model that could be considered the nearest in its ideals and aims to those of an FPE, we may find one in Summerhill School or the Sudbury Valley Schools, which already have several years of experience in applying the principles of freedom closely connected to rules of responsibility. It is therefore interesting to see if and how far the daily life of a student, and the internal administration of a new school and university, might be inspired by that model.

First of all, it should be said that there are no hierarchical figures, there are no 'directors', 'presidents', or higher ranking personalities with more administrative powers. There could be single figures which have some special task or responsibility, but everyone is subject to the rule of laws enacted by the General Assembly.

General Assembly: The General Assembly (GA) is the committee which takes decisions relevant to the administration and life of the FPS, FPH or FPU, making them, through a process of direct democracy, self-administered institutions. Each institution is represented by all the enrolled students and learning mentors. All have the right of one vote. Participation is open to all members, but is not compulsory. The GA handles all the issues of the school or university and their internal life, i.e. it deals with ideas, plans, applications, problems, rules, financial issues, household, and develops common solutions, and decides what learning mentors are allowed to be hired or not, who is allowed to take part in the community, and who must go. It is in this context that the students must comply with its rules and directives. In the case of serious breaches of rules by students, or anyone else, the offenders could be dismissed by the GA. In fact, the GA decides on the hiring and dismissal of the staff, the financial issues like the renewal of the buildings, their maintenance, and the financing of projects, lectures or other activities related to the life of the institution. The GA discusses, votes on, and ratifies the internal regulations, as well as their modification. In case of conflicts or breaches of the rules, it can set up a legal committee which discusses the cases in order to find compromises and resolve conflicts. It can, if other options did not produce results, impose sanctions and penalties. The GA is the administrative heart of the school or university.

Communication Committee: It manages all the contacts and the communication policies with the outside world. The communication committee is subject to the GA. Its task is that of organizing PR, marketing and fund-raising campaigns. It builds up the presence of the FPE entreprise on the Internet (i.e. through websites, Facebook, blogs, Twitter, etc.). During the initial phase, a pre-marketing action is probably necessary, with seminars, conferences, and information evenings, and recourse to the Internet, in order to convey to the public the benefits of the free-progress concept and its methods.

Students: Anyone can enrol in an FPS, FPH or FPU. As already stated, age, sex, and disability should not be criteria for acceptance, and the 'first come, first served' rule should apply. It should be made perfectly clear to all concerned that responsibility comes with freedom. Every student and, equally, every learning mentor and every member of staff, will be subject to the rules set by the GA. Non-compliance with the rules and decisions ratified by the GA will lead to disciplinary action, including dismissal.

Learning mentors: These are trained employees with diverse professional backgrounds and academic skills that have an extensive know-how in a range of subjects. They differ from traditional teachers and professors, by their pedagogical and didactic skills, which are characterized by a high degree of clarity, empathy, and sensitivity. Their task is to help students to discover their true and innate talents, skills, and abilities in order to pursue the research direction that best fits them. A learning mentor does not command, but helps. He is not allowed to impose a prescribed curriculum, exercises, learning material, or laboratory activity, but helps in setting the goals and in the project selection. Students agree with the learning mentor on what they want to learn. Their task is to help the students in finding information. The learning mentor can, upon request, recommend methods about how the student may assimilate the teaching material, and can keep teaching courses or even make test and examinations, but only upon request or when the interests of the students themselves demand such action. The learning mentors are hired or fired by the students themselves or by the GA, which decides anyway about their employment. Periodic meetings can be held to consider whether particular learning mentors are to be confirmed in their position or shown the door. While they might be part-time or full-time employees, they should not expect to be entitled to a civil-servant status.

Contact person: Belongs to the communications committee, and officially represents outwardly the FPS, FPH or FPU. He/she is elected by the GA, and reports to it. The contact person is not a 'director' of the institute or a professional figure in a leading position, since such a figure does not exist in the first place.

External specialists: When required, external specialists can be hired to hold specifically oriented education courses, or because of their special skills that are not covered by learning mentors.

Projects: Projects should always be initiated by students themselves. It is the students who decide on the content of their own project, and they also fully accept responsibility for the outcome of their work. While learning mentors may propose a specific study or research project, they will have no say in deciding who takes up the project, or how it is to be handled.

Learning groups: These should come into being spontaneously, during everyday life. A free and spontaneous collective co-creative cooperation is also produced by self-initiated projects, the learning mentors are available upon request, with their knowledge and skills, to advise and help in this formation.

External degrees: In the free-progress system of education, there are no certificates, degrees, or diplomas. Typically, a student completes his/her course with the production of a development portfolio, a thesis, or an intellectual product. However, it is open to a student to ask for an external exam that will lead to a certificate from an external school or academic institution. The learning mentor concerned will assist the student through this process as well.

Facility Manager: Takes care of the bureaucracy, the management of finances (according to the regulations of the GA), and the maintenance of the structures.

Financing: The school or university is financed by donations, sponsors, foundations, grants, etc.

Student self-financing: Students work within a budget they have designed themselves. Items covered are their living expenses and costs of studies, including those of equipment, participation in workshops and congresses, travel, and external courses. The budget preparation has the twin advantages, namely independence from top-down funding pressures that are common in traditional academic institutions, and actual experience of responsibility in managing finances.

Sociocracy (98) could be the other possible alternative form of governance. It is also called 'dynamic governance'. Sociocracy goes beyond democracy, and relies on the idea that there are better ways to make decisions and to find common solutions than imposing the result of an election or referendum from one opinion group onto another. In fact, democracy after all still contains several aspects of the authoritarian mindset inherently. There are the winners (the majority) and the losers (the minority). The latter have to obey decisions they may not agree with, while the latter rule against their will. Finally an element of coercion remains.

Democracy is still a linear system, where the power flows one way, whereas, in dynamic systems, the power flows back and forth between all the elements that make up the group, or institution, or social system.

In what sense does sociocracy differ from democracy? The difference between the two notions lies in the greater scope sociocracy offers to open discussions between members of a (hierarchical or non-hierarchical) system. The members form groups, and take up problems of concern for discussion. Creative solutions emerge from the deliberations that ensue, and will have the advantage of spontaneous consent, something that cannot be claimed for a top-down system, or for a scenario in which the majority vote wins. This so because a recommendation or decision that is the outcome of a debate in which all the parties concerned have participated will, obviously, reflect the views of all of them. All the levels of the hierarchy are involved in the policy making of an organization. That is, sociocracy is based on the 'consent' of all (not consensus which is based on 'one man, one vote'). Consent is realized after a debate which tries to find a mutually acceptable solution that meets the interests of all the members and that are served equally. Dynamic governance relies on the interaction between these 'circles', that is, the group of people of a department, team or division, and that make policy decisions together on an equivalent basis by consent decision methods (of course, in a conventional enterprise these departments exist too, but they usually do not have much say or decision making power, and if they do, the minority will have to succumb to the majority). Consent is obtained by 'rounds' where everyone can object and, most importantly, make amendments through proposals which indicate novel, creative and original solutions which were previously not thought of, and that may satisfy all the members (contrary to the conventional democratic decision making process, where frequently one stops short before a consent and forces consensus). However, it is conceivable that in certain situations consent may not materialize, and consensus then appears the only available recourse. Only as a last extreme measure, if consent did not result, even after several rounds, consensus is applied. This might look at first a very time consuming process, but experience shows that it did save frequently a system from collapsing. Unanimous decisions are difficult to obtain, but work if there is willingness to propose alternatives and compromise, and a precise regulated set of rules are enacted which determine the rounds, the objections and listening dynamics. The key is to transform a crisis from a spiral of complaints coming from the base which criticizes the top for its failures, to a flat hierarchy dynamics where the base has the power to offer alternative, constructive and creative proposals that suggest a way out of the crises, and a common framing of the collective future. It is about a 'circle' process: sociocracy distinguishes between a 'general circle' and the 'top circle', each with different figures in charge and eventually structured hierarchically (but not necessarily so), with each level linked by having representatives of the lower level to the upper level, and with veto power. It is a form of equalitarian cooperation on a team based decision making by consent towards a common goal. As an example of the effectiveness of sociocracy the case of Gerard Endenburg's electrical engineering company is cited frequently. Due to a deep financial crisis in the 1970's, he was almost forced to close or lay off sixty workers. However, through a system regulated by a dynamic governance of consent, the creative process led to the idea that the sixty workers could be quickly trained for another job, i.e. marketing, which led to the growth of several departments and the solution of all the problems in three months. Endenburg's company became the world's first sociocratic self-owned organization, abolishing thereby the owner-employee relationship. And, by the way, to connect to the above mentioned Kodak's bankruptcy case, one might wonder if the company's trajectory would have been different if its corporate structure had been sociocratic instead of a top-down hierarchy? Sociocracy is still in its infancy, but so far it has been implemented successfully in several business enterprises, organizations, and also some schools, like for instance the Rainbow Mountain Childerns School (RMCS). (99)

Possible research areas of a Free-Progress-University

In principle, if we really wished to be consistent with the ideals of an FPU, the question of what kind of research areas should be pursued in a free-progress university should not even arise: a free-progress academy must develop spontaneously, without there being already in advance established departments and intellectual lines of inquiry. Areas of research are identified by the learning community, i.e. the students and the learning mentors. However, it might be interesting, at least at a speculative level, to try to put forward some suggestions which might serve to encourage and stimulate newcomers to pursue some study in one or the other subject. Because, there are several lines of research, topics and interests that are usually not allowed inside the current academic paths, since they are too far away from the mainstream thinking or the accepted conventional ideas.

New education research, in the form of new pedagogical and didactical concepts, tools, and practices, might well become one of the central studies of an FPU. Of course, pedagogical studies are not new as such, as school teachers (who must take exams and practical tests before being allowed to teach) know very well. But the science of education explored in a completely different setting such as an FPU would acquire a wholly new dimension and meaning. The research on new didactical and pedagogical approaches inside a really free university will give us completely new insights. An FPU will become a test bed in practice of many educational theories which were previously impossible to verify in an authoritarian learning system.

Peace, conflict resolution, and self-determination studies could also find in an FPU an ideal place to flourish. It is hard to understand why, in a world plagued by wars and civil unrests, these lines of research are still so scarce in academia. It is incredible that, while the world is filled with weapons of mass destruction, where military spending is seen to be rising, terrorism and ethnic tensions are constantly increasing in a globalized world, peace studies and conflict resolution topics in the academic world remain much too limited. They do not exist in most universities, and where they do, they occupy a tiny niche in research. This is probably due to the fact that these are still relatively new lines of inquiry, and as in the case of everything that is new, they are treated with scepticism and doubt. In a hierarchal system, students are not allowed to propose new themes, and all themes must be approved by professors who may already have chosen another direction, and have something else in mind, it will take years, if not generations, to slip through new research directions in line with the times. In an FPU, this problem does not arise. It is inherently encoded in its essence that students themselves propose new lines of research without needing approval by anyone, and it even encourages them to do so.

New world economy, ecology, sustainability, and fair trade are becoming increasingly urgent topics. However, in most institutions, these are still learned and taught with a basically conventional capitalistic mindset that puts at centre stage the GNP, mere liquidity indicators, and the exploitation of human and natural resources. Still too scarce are efforts in designing new principles which rely on genuine progress, the common well-being, or respect for the preservation of natural resources. Is it just a vain chimera, a too idealistic wishful thinking to conceive of a just economy and trade? Could there be other leading principles than egoism, competitiveness, and material appropriation without ethics that can guide world economy?

New foundations of physics research could be another possible line of inquiry. Applied physics experienced a tremendous development when several new discoveries from the micro- to macro-cosmos were made. But while the theory of relativity, quantum physics, and the standard model (SM) of particle physics that emerged from it revolutionized our worldview of the physical world, the past half-century has not seen much progress in the conceptual foundations of theoretical physics. Relativity and quantum mechanics are both correct theories, and yet they seem conceptually incompatible. Relativity describes well the force of gravity, but seems to have nothing to do with electromagnetic and nuclear forces. Quantum mechanics describes well the latter forces, and even unifies them, but refuses to encompass gravity. It is known that, even though it is an extraordinarily successful and tested theory, the SM can't be the whole story, because it contains several free and yet fine-tuned arbitrary parameters, apparently just by an extraordinary coincidence. But any attempt to go beyond these theories has so far failed. Generations of physicists worldwide have tried to conceive of a new 'quantum gravity theory', but such attempts have only led to an even deeper crisis, since most of these theories turned out to be either wrong or far beyond any possibility to be experimentally tested in the foreseeable future. Slowly but steadily, it is becoming clear that the problem might not be only of a technical nature, but perhaps has its roots in an encrusted way of conceiving the material world. New ideas, insights, and original, groundbreaking intuitions are necessary to get out of the impasse. What is missing in our present social and academic structures are the 'seers' who, like Copernicus, Galileo, Newton, or Einstein, understand the fallacies of the conventional paradigm, and are able to look further. Only then will we probably be able to go beyond the present crisis of theoretical physics. But, as we have seen in the previous sections, these are precisely the kind of personalities that the present colleges and universities refuse to admit. An FPU instead would be an ideal place where they could express themselves.

These were only some examples of possible lines of research in an FPU. It is quite possible that completely new lines will turn up. These examples were only meant to highlight how several research areas may find a much vaster and more fertile ground in an FPU mileau than in conventional universities.

The social and infrastructural foundations for a Free-Progress-Learning self-developing Campus

The architectonic disposition of modern colleges speaks volumes about the lack of an interdisciplinary mindset. Every department has its building. The architectonic compartmentalization is a reflection of the cultural compartmentalization. This division may have practical advantages, but there is an unnoticed drawback. Philosophers of science rarely share their time with scientists outside seminars for the simple reason that they are physically separated. The same can be said of physicians and biologists, or artists and scientists, and so on. But a real living and culturally dynamic environment should not have these artificial segmentations. We should recall how the great philosophers and natural scientists of ancient Greece considered it a perfectly natural fact that artists, philosophers, scientists, and others could talk, interact, and exchange their knowledge and experience with one another. Interaction between people of very different backgrounds can ignite a diversity of ideas and new forms of collaboration that would not be possible if they were housed in widely separate structures.

Whereas the way we interpret the department compartmentalization in a conventional academic setting should be submitted to a critical assessment. System theory, the study of how complex systems work, can help us understand what is problematic in the fragmentation of a university system into separate and distinct departments and sub-departments. A university, college or school structure, with all its social activities, should be considered a complex system of human interactions. According to system theory, a healthy and functioning complex system is always a whole of interrelated and interdependent parts which cannot be divided into independent parts. Considering these parts as independent units in isolation from the others cannot explain the properties of this very same whole. This is because each of its parts determines and affects the properties and behavior of the whole, which arise due to its mutual interactions. For example, a human being cannot be considered merely a combination of independent organs. The properties and the behavior of a complex system like a living organism are the result of the interdependent interactions of each of its organs. Furthermore, the quality and improvement of each part does not necessarily improve the whole; eventually, it may worsen its efficiency and eventually kill it. This can be exemplified by the example of how a car works. Assembling the best automotive parts from different cars and different automobile companies won't result in the creation of the best car. This is because the parts simply don't fit, as they are made for very different systems. Instead, it is the way the parts fit together – and not how they perform separately – that determines the performance and efficiency of the whole system.

This might sound almost obvious to us were it not for the fact that this is precisely what we (more or less unconsciously) suddenly ignore in shaping an educational system. We break up our universities, colleges and schools into independent departments, curricula and programs, trying to manage each one independently based on the assumption that the optimization of each of these separate departments, curricula and programs will optimize the whole as well as possible. How this unconscious assumption permeates our mindset was made eloquently clear in a famous system thinking speech by Russell Ackoff, an American organizational theorist (100). According to system thinking principles, a part should not be modified unless it makes the whole better. Each change of a part must take into account its impact on the whole. Therefore, one should conceive of an educational system as a complex living organism, nor as an entity made of independently performing pieces. One should not try to improve the performance of a single department unless one can't prove that this will improve the performance of the university as a whole.

Unfortunately, we conceive of an educational institution anti-systemically, treating it as being made of a group of autonomous independent units called 'university departments' and, in schools, as strictly age-structured classrooms, each with its own separate and independent curricula and programs, without conceiving of it as an integral part of the whole. That is also the deeper reason why half a century of attempts to foster and incentivize so-called 'interdisciplinarity' did not succeed. Once we separate the system into independent disciplines, we can't bring them back together again. Once the glass is broken, you can't pretend to get it back with a time machine. If one creates a system considering the parts only as independent fundamental constituents, the system loses most of its real inherent potentialities. We should, instead, conceive of and design a complex system, like an FPE environment, moving from the whole to the parts so that the whole is dealt with before the parts are created to fit the whole.

For this reason, in the new educational paradigm, the architectonic paradigm changes too: the office of a physicist should be just near that of an artist, or a philosopher, or a biologist. At the same time, it makes no sense to lump everything together indiscriminately. The laboratory of a physicist needs very different instrumentation than that of a biologist or chemist, a music hall must be isolated acoustically from other rooms, an academy of fine arts will need a very different environment than that of those who are going to practise physical activity in a sports hall, the students looking for a class in maths will need a lecture hall other than that of those learning a foreign language, etc.

However, first and foremost, we should question if it makes sense at all to reproduce all these facilities from scratch every time a new campus is built.

The complex where the individual learning process and the educational path is lived in a daily practice focusing on one's own diverse interests, that is, on a specific subject or topic, must not necessarily occur in a centralized space. A theatre or music hall can be offered by a municipality. A library too. A laboratory of an already existing university, research centre, or any other institution could be lent to a group of students, conceiving it as some cultural exchange. Sports fields exist almost everywhere, also in the smallest towns, and do not need to be build all over again for a special educational purpose. In most cities, craftwork facilities or painting halls can be rented and do not need to exist on a new campus. Many other examples of this kind could be made. The question is if it makes really sense to rebuild all these structures, centralizing them in a single campus when they stand at disposal anyway. Could we not conceive an infrastructurally decentralized education that can, at least in part, take advantage of the structures that already exist in its surroundings?

It is not necessary to 're-invent the wheel' all the time. Museums, swimming pools, expositions, and cultural events already exist out there and are only waiting to be visited. It is time to also free children and students physically from that suffocating and centralized material building we call 'school'. The fact that we take it for granted that every school and university must necessarily have all these infrastructures in one place, cramming children and students in the same geographical location, reflects our homogenizing and centralising mentality. But mentalities can and should change.

On the other hand, some kind of central infrastructure that allows children, students, and mentors to meet in a place (and that eventually also offers shelter) remains an inescapable necessity for a healthy learning environment. A social factor remains and will forever be part of the human character because it is also true that people learn best when they learn together. Eliminating the free social interaction that arises among students of a campus or among like-minded people who have a common goal or project would cause harm, or severely limit the potentiality that such a collective has to offer. Therefore, while single educational practices or studies could be shifted to external geographically decentralized structures, a meeting and living centre remains desirable nevertheless.

A common sector could serve the purpose of nurturing continuing interaction between students of different disciplines and subjects. This central unit will accommodate school children and high-school and university students. Care will be taken to ensure that, to the extent possible, and without distinction of age, students are enabled to form their own study group, project, class or individually self-determined learning path. To this end, project rooms will be provided, equipped to meet the requirements of each group, including a laboratory if needed. A large public hall with an annexed social meeting place could be located amid gardens and may play a role in immediate information exchange between different groups or just as a relaxation and socialisation place in students' free time. This common structure must not be devoid of educational and activity structures that are needed on a daily basis. Several small study rooms for group activities and a larger study hall for personal silent study sessions could be useful. There would be a state-of-the-art computer room with broadband Internet. The instructors, mentors, and other helpers would have their own offices. The parts of this structure would be integrated, and not differentiated by subject or discipline or study theme. Also, a distinct administrative and residential zone form a unit. Here are located the secretaries and bureaucratic facilities as also dormitories and accommodation structures for students, such as a refectory and a cafe. Learning, teaching and creative activity in an open-air setting, ideally in a natural environment, should be available so that students no longer spend all day sitting in closed rooms. The contact with nature and fresh air resulting from more physical movement and exercise not only favors physical health but fosters psychological wellbeing, clarity of mind and intuitive thinking.

Moreover, since the FPE paradigm relies on an age-crossing learning environment, we should also ask, how far does a separation among the different educational systems make sense any longer? Nowadays we think in terms of a hierarchic educational structure and take it for granted that one has to first attend primary-, secondary- and high schools, then eventually go to college and university and finally be promoted to an academic post-doctoral scientist in a research centre. Of course, even in a FPE learning environment, it is to be expected that the Nobel laureate professor of a FPU will spend much more of his/her time with adults who can grasp the complex issues of a state of the art discipline, than with a 6-year-old child who still can't read and write and is spending his time on the playground of a democratic Sudbury-Valley styled school. But there is no necessity to impose this educational segmentation a priori. We should allow a spontaneous gathering among all the different levels of intellectual maturity, preparation and interest of each child, student and adult. There is no reason to erect conceptual and physical walls between so-called primary- and 'higher education'. This doesn't mean that this distinction no longer exists, but that it is perfectly possible to conceive of an environment that allows them to co-exist without separations. What speaks against a free-progress-campus where a 65-year-old FPU professor shares his/her daily professional life and wisdom in the same learning infrastructure of a 16-year-old student of a FPH or a 6-year-old child of a democratic school? That would not be limiting, but potentially even be very enriching for all.

Therefore, the structure of a 'free-progress learning campus' might look like as follows.

Free Progress Campus

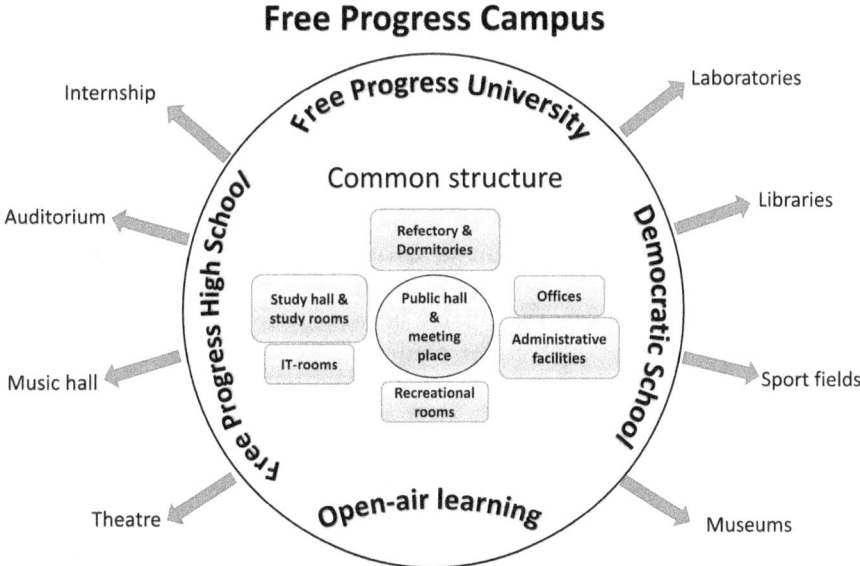

However, it is not the architecture with its infrastructures as such which is supposed to be different than any other, but it is the kind of social foundation of the learning and teaching practices which it tries to optimize that is distinctive. There are no (or not necessarily) subjects, classes or faculties like maths, history, languages, chemistry, biology, philosophy, etc., but just projects and eventually a 'faculty' or course designed by the student or a group of students with self-styled curricula and syllabus. There is no compulsion to choose a specialization and one might develop a multi- and inter-disciplinary learning path or research. On the other hand, there is no compulsion to avoid specialization either. If someone likes to devote his/her own time to the study of a particular topic, there should be no barriers. A project room and a laboratory could serve the purpose, which also means that there are no classrooms in the sense of a teacher-centred instruction (even though that might still exist, if requested by the child or student). There are no departments either, at least not in their traditional meaning, but only places where the individual or groups of individuals meet and foster their own intellectual development and growth by initiating open ended learning paths and lines of research which are not pre-ordered in content or in time. The role of mentors as teachers should however not be underestimated. If they desire to offer a course or a project, that can be offered to the community. There should be no restraints either.

If we look at things from this perspective, the campus becomes a very different place compared to standard schools or conventional university structures. There are no strict compartmentalisations in the form of departments, faculties, curricula and timetables. Or, if there are, they are lived externally, and yet maintaining the identity of the scholar as part of a community.

Such a free-progress campus, regulated by a democratic or sociocratic administrative principle, spontaneous cooperation, and project-based learning models is a social structure evolutionary in character. It does not need so much continuous reforms dictated from the top of a hierarchy of teachers or professors or a political establishment which has permanently to discuss with endless controversies before it can ratify what children should learn and what subjects or faculties should be taught to keep up with the challenges of the time. Such a structure is a living organism which self-reforms, innovates, improves, changes and reorganizes itself on a daily basis, because there are no constraints on student's changes in interests, inclinations and to what people could do and should learn. Adaptation to social changes and new necessities or interest of the collective will come naturally as soon its members perceive this to be necessary by reshaping and adjusting their own learning and research direction and pathway. Simply because this is a transformation which each individual, or group of individuals, is free to determine and is no longer subject to approval from a higher hierarchy of a collective. In this sense it is all about a completely new educational and social structure which determines a different conception of how an intellectual and social growth should occur. It is not determined by the constraints and commands neither of a collective nor of an individual, but by a free progress of a self-developing Unity in Diversity.

What the daily life in a Free-Progress-School & University might look like

It must be emphasized that FPE is not only focused on an "in-person centered" path which allows everybody to handcraft his/her own curriculum, but wants also to go beyond that by offering young students, who are nowadays bound to conventional institutions, a viable and realistic alternative option that replaces the standard faculty, that is, the division within a university or college comprising one subject area.

Of course, one can learn complex topics first by browsing specific areas of interest and only later deciding whether to go deeper by focusing on the basics. However, if someone wants to become a professional, focusing on first principles and learning the (sometimes boring) basics will sooner or later become an unavoidable step in the cognitive process. If one wants to go beyond a hobby-styled interest and learn how to engineer complex devices or develop new theories, learning the basics and the first principles is necessary.

As an example I can personally speak of, someone who wants to learn physics at a professional level must first learn math (calculus, linear algebra, and several other mathematical methods), then learn at least classical mechanics, electromagnetism, relativity, thermodynamics and quantum mechanics. Each of these require a long course and an intense preparation which inevitably necessitates a period of learning the basics and the development of an intellectual background where personal speculations must be set aside for a while. Only then one can say to have a background comparable to a 'normal' graduate student and is able to begin to see the 'global picture' of a quite complex science, which otherwise remains cryptic and almost unintelligible.

A fixed universal sequence must not necessarily exist. Indeed, there is a subjective element to what must be learned first and what must be learned later. However, sciences such as math and physics are structured in levels of complexity: one cannot understand quantum theory if the math, such as the concepts of classical mechanics and electromagnetism, isn't mastered first. This does not imply that we must go back to the good old one-way professor-centered lecture with exams, grades and certificates. But this knowledge and these skills cannot be acquired without taking into account a curriculum which is suggested by an experienced advisor (and must look somewhat further than the motto "life is my school", as so several unschoolers like to declare).

Therefore, we must conceive of a possible daily life learning track in a FPU where the 'person-centered' path is complemented by a "faculty-centered" path, and yet without falling again into compulsory and authoritarian tendencies.

There are several possible self-directed learning contexts that would make this possible. For example, the following graph shows a conceptual structure on which the flip teaching method combined with a competence portfolio-based learning could serve this purpose.

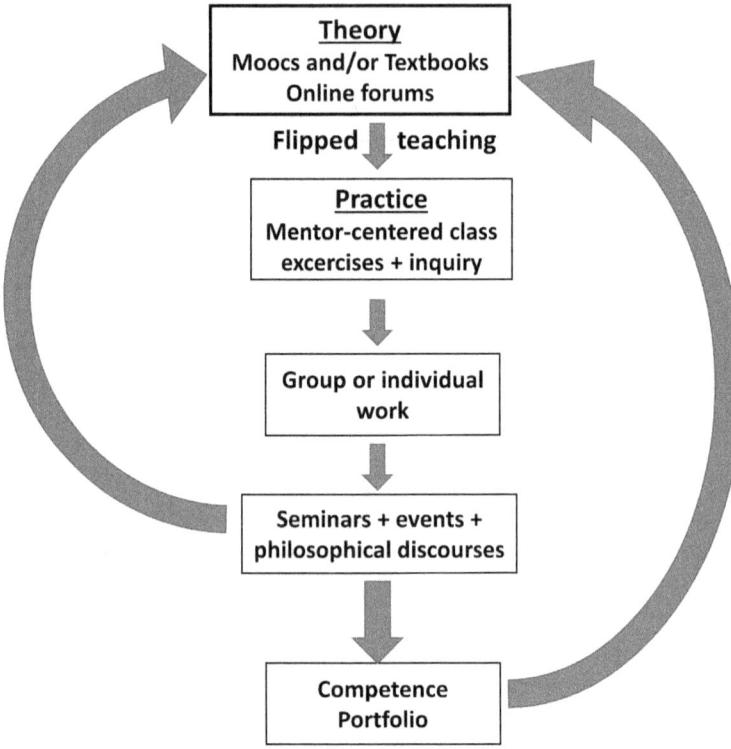

First, students follow the single lectures on the theoretical aspects of a subject via an online course, which could be chosen from among the world's best MOOCs. In addition or alternatively, students teach themselves as autodidacts with standard textbooks or other printed media which are considered the best-structured and intelligible documents by the advisor, the community or eventually recommended by the students of the previous courses themselves.

During this phase, first issues and questions may arise that could be discussed preliminarily in an online forum section. Here, students can interact with each other and/or with the advisor, discussing things in a written format online as a means of preparing for the elaboration that will occur in the next phase.

Once the students have gone through this theoretical session represented by the single lecture (which replaces the teacher- or professor centered lecture), they physically meet together to put into practice, with the help of an advisor, what was discussed in the online video. This is then the common and shared practical part of the day. After this mentor-centered class, a learning effort in the form of exercises or repetition may follow. This can be made alone, at home, or with study groups in the study hall & rooms offered by the free-progress-campus infrastructure. A living and learning community should not only learn from videos or books but should be able to enjoy a more dynamic cultural exchange with others on state-of-the-art and up-to-date topics by participating in seminars, events, workshops, etc., that should be considered as a natural appendix to the daily life in a FPU.

This flip teaching cycle will repeat itself until the last lecture of the course. Then, at the point in time where conventional institutions ask for an exam and give grades, in a FPU this is replaced by asking students to deliver a little research or manufacture a material or intellectual product of their own, and which attests how the course has enhanced their competence in the specific subject and which then will go into their competence portfolio. Even this cycle can be repeated again until the same competence and degree of knowledge of a conventional university faculty division is acquired.

More in general, what would the daily life in an FPS, FPH and FPU look like? All of the following activities could be conceived. At first sight, they might not look much different from the traditional college life. But what distinguishes them from the old way of conceiving the academic daily life is their completely free character. All students are encouraged to participate, but no one is compelled to be present.

- The studies take place in the study rooms or at MOOCs individually and/or in groups (e.g. by SOLE, DPPBL, LdL teaching methods, etc.). Learning mentors assist, but students are not obligated to appoint any.
- Participation in seminars and courses which can be held both by learning mentors or by students themselves. Participation should never be compulsory.

- Project management: individual and collective processing and implementation of plans. Projects are first proposed by the students.
- Barcamps and student-initiated Group Formation Camps.
- Delivering presentations that make the work of the individual or the group known to the rest of the learning community.
- Periodic voluntary GA sessions.
- Participation at conferences, creation of posters, and talks. Mentors can advise but which congresses, workshops, and conferences to attend, as the content of the poster and/or the talks is only left to the students.
- Study experience in other institutions and/or abroad (e.g. in the style of the European mobility for students like Erasmus).
- Open Day.
- Party time!

The vision of a University of Human Unity[4]

The above FPE paradigm inspired by such a didactical, administrative and infrastructural frame is based on true democratic principles, eventually guided by sociocratic means of systemic consensus and focused on the potential of the individual inside a larger unity in diversity, also suggests a culturally international, all-embracing structure. One can envisage a futuristic educational environment that goes beyond the borders of nations and the culture of its people yet maintains single peculiarities and national spirt inside a larger unity. A facility where students from the same country could live inside their own communities while interacting, studying and living with students of other countries. An education center from kindergarten to graduate and post-graduate classes with hostel-type residential buildings to accommodate visitors of all faiths and nationalities from all over the world.

There would be a section for every country added by national pavilions of the diverse nations, representing their cultures, civilizations and traditions. Diverse blocks not demarcated by walls but by the free development of their own pattern of life so that if students want to know a

---

[4] The concept of a 'University of Human Unity' was largely inspired by the vision of Mirra Alfassa. Refer to the endnote of the book for more details.

particular way of life, they can straightaway walk into the respective sector and mix with the students there. Also, an international museum is proposed to be built where students and visitors will find a display of the different civilizations of the world, past and present, with, for example, artists from various countries giving expression to their national life. Each nation and its distinctive culture, true nature, genius, qualities and mission in the terrestrial concert could be displayed and should make its own contribution to a cultural synthesis. A permanent 'world-exhibition' that will present all countries in a concrete and living way. Students would live and study together in this international context in a multidisciplinary fashion through creative trans-national interaction in a permanent meeting place. This cultural synthesis will be found in a university through the concept of the ancient Pythagorean school, as well as through the cultures of different regions of the earth present onsite and represented in a way that is accessible to all, not merely intellectually but also in terms of habits, customs and art.

This World Education & Research Center could begin with a residential international university which, by becoming a cultural center for the synthesis of different knowledges and skills, would become the representation of a small-scale 'world-union' in an attempt to set the foundation for a fairer, brighter and nobler life for mankind in its extreme diversities though bound together by an inner unity.

It should be clear that in such a University of Human Unity, students are not participating because they want to attain a degree for a job which allows them to make a living. The students, as well as the learning mentors, will receive what is necessary for their subsistence, but won't get monetary compensation for their service. Behind such a non-commercial international learning setting stands a higher purpose of cooperation and collaboration based on mutual goodwill and growth of consciousness instead of a struggle against each other guided by a separative, stern discipline.

The aim is to nurture an ideal of human unity instead of the global competition which is nowadays so cherished. Education will be free and open to all boys and girls, men and women from all over the world regardless of race, nationality, faith or culture. No department of knowledge, discipline or research will be left out. Languages, science, philosophy, arts and all humanities and sciences in all their theoretical and practical facets, physical or metaphysical, are to be taught, learned, practiced and researched. The growth of human knowledge and the creation of an enlightened youth and humanity will be the guiding motives. Students may also be allowed to receive instruction in their own language.

Pupils in Kindergarten and researchers at the post-graduate level from all nations will live and learn side by side. However, sections grouped according to nationality are allowed, such that a single culture, language and social life can be lived within a larger framework of communal life. The way of life will be neither western nor eastern, but will include the best of both and will seek to go beyond it, towards something that can hardly be presently imagined.

If people from all different countries and cultures meet like this at the intellectual and spiritual level, it could become a small-scale testbed for a world-university that fosters a world-unity on the basis of a human Unity and Oneness in the multiplicity and diversity. A Unity of the human race that goes beyond the external association of economic or intellectual interests and that meets, as a larger life, at the level of an inner spiritual Oneness. Not a mere copy of other universities or research centers abroad, where thousands of students just pass out, but a synthetic organisation of all nations, each occupying its true place according to its own genius and the part it plays in the whole, aspiring to build a new personality in a new World. It aims to be a place where people can enter the depths of their own being, where mind and reason are not the last word, where people can live from within outwards. An ambiance where the collective and the individual meet and are no longer in contradiction; to the contrary, they both are indispensable conditions for the progress of the whole. A collective reorganisation in which all individuals encounter the conditions that allow them to freely work towards a progressive evolution of mankind.

Once this multi-cultural university – in the form of a miniature cooperative world community based on an FPE paradigm – succeeds in harmoniously accommodating all its diverse cultures and national identities, a further step could be taken. Being autonomous and strictly non-political in character, the university could also serve as a mediator and conciliator between nations, cultures or ethnic identities in conflict. It lends itself naturally to serving as an ideal playground for new peace and conflict resolution projects via a dialogue that encourages a greater sense of international awareness and responsibility.

This latter aspect might close the circle we began to trace in our long journey by analysing the education concepts from the age of enlightenment and which led us to the futuristic ideal of an FPE. Education in its conventional understanding, as it has so far been practiced, has not led to peace, nor has it led humanity to a higher harmony and mutual understanding. Quite the contrary. The people who are in charge and who start wars are not the illiterate and ignorant. Dictators and fanatic extremists as Islamic terrorists turned out to be, most of the time, the rich and well-trained minds who sometimes even received the best education from internationally renowned schools and colleges. This is because education was – and still is – considered a strictly intellectual and factual exercise that fosters only the rational thinking and logical skills useful for the economic and material growth of society, but which leaves out the entire spectrum of the inner spiritual and intuitive dimension of the human being. It is quite natural that a learning environment riddled with fear of examinations and grades, with pupils and youngsters who, instead of being treated as seeds that bear, within the entire plant, all its leaves, flowers and fruits, instead considers them to be blank pages and forces them to learn from outdated curricula and syllabuses which have no relation to the real world, cannot lead them to live freely and harmoniously with others or themselves. It is almost obvious that this approach, which disallows the following of one's own inclinations and inspirations and the pursuit of happiness, has produced a 'spiritual illiteracy' that does not foster empathy and acceptance of diversity in children, who ultimately won't be able to regulate conflicts as grown-ups because they won't allow the same for others.

The only entity that can succeed in doing otherwise is an educational environment that promotes the free development of the human mind and that is devoid of compulsion on children, who will learn to live – and live to learn – freely and harmoniously with themselves and others. Living with people of diverse cultural backgrounds who join together to work for the development of all – for instance, by working on an international program for restoring humankind's lost equilibrium with Nature – can lead us to a real peace which is not just the absence of war or an external economic and political arrangement. Ultimately, the real problem is not so much knowing what to do but knowing how to be.

The short- and long-term aims

"If I had asked people what they wanted, they would have said faster horses."
Henry Ford

Finally, a few words about the short- and long-term aims.

The short-term aim is the necessity to ignite a spark which works as an overall beginning. That's how peaceful revolutions came frequently into being. From little things which go in the right direction and that grow with time passing by. But these little things were not just dreams and theories but also and especially some form of doing and action. It would be of no use to build or acquire land and material infrastructures if they could not be filled already with living souls who are impatient to work and practise. Otherwise, these structures would remain only empty and lifeless cathedrals. Today, I see so many young people joining and discussing together the future of higher education. They imagine, speculate and conjecture what that could be, but usually no clear ideas emerge, there are many more questions than answers. However, as life experience shows, these answers come with time and by initiating a practice and an action which plants the seed of something that could grow. The only practical beginning that goes beyond a mere debate is that people come together at a place where to study, initiate projects, form study groups, read, learn and teach. What is learned should not be only for one's own sake but something from which a community could profit almost immediately or at least already in the early stages of the learning process. Meeting, doing research, working together on projects and presenting it to the community in one form or another is the first necessary triggering spark. Discussing alone what and how to practise a new paradigm cannot be enough. Equally important are the topics, their extensions, and the professional level they reach. Of course, in an FPE environment, everyone is free to work on any subject and topic desired. However, as I have seen in many instances, initiating a cookery course or knitting and sewing classes on weekends won't work, not even as a seed. It stagnates again. If an FPH or an FPU are to come into existence, their members must sooner or later come to accept that a long-term engagement with high-level topics or research areas is going to have to be addressed. The same goes for those who want to teach. A single seminar during the holiday season will not help make an FPU. What is needed are fully fledged seasonal courses as yearlong schooling and academic paths that will train and develop knowledge and skills. This will contribute to helping students produce material that would go into their portfolios. This is about going beyond a notion of alternative higher education as marginally more than a leisure-time activity.

Over the long term, the aim will be to provide to students knowledge and qualification that will be recognized beyond the free-progress institution's walls. It will be knowledge and qualification acquired through a completely different learning paradigm to the familiar paradigm. The level of understanding and competence a free-progress alumnus/alumna shows in his/her subject should be comparable to, or higher than, those seen in students from conventional educational institutions. It is not simply about a school or university which offers some course as an appendix, as an added chunk of knowledge to students of present conventional institutions, but a complete, self-contained academic structure that is aimed at. What is wrong with present schools and university faculties is not so much what they teach but how they force people to study it. A mature, fully fledged FPS and campus should be a living example which shows the world that things can be done otherwise and better than in the present learning formats. In this sense, it should offer the possibility to students who express the desire to enrol in a faculty, say in some faculty of arts, science, medicine, engineering, philosophy, history, or whatever, the same or similar academic skills as are available in the conventional educational system. When they graduate, they will have the same or even better preparation with a vaster and deeper understanding that they can use in the rest of the world, which might look upon it first with scepticism, but with time will recognize it.

Once this learning paradigm is established and is seen to work, it can be proposed as a platform, a laboratory of universal education that the world can look upon as an alternative to the present-day, old-fashioned, and strictly intellectual educational systems. A platform where other students, teachers, and professors from around the world can be invited to experience how it is possible to eliminate the present division between learning and self-directed learning, understanding and intuition, knowledge and inspiration.

Conclusion

I guess that, at least in the Western world of our times, less than half of the population does jobs that have real social value. Few jobs, professions, and careers produce goods or services of social usefulness that serve to promote a common material, cultural, or psychological state of wellbeing. In the best case, these jobs are simply void occupations that leave no trace. But most are also detrimental to society and the environment as a whole. They are directed towards the production of unnecessary or unhealthy consumer goods, or serve small financial or academic elites, or favour a system which destroys the natural habitat. We still live under the illusion that the energy we put into our job is good for the community. Our culture, our mental categories, and especially our educational and economic system, are such that the vast majority of us work a job that is unnecessary, or even harmful, for the collective benefit, and, moreover, does in no way describe or determine who we are as a person. These jobs – namely, those jobs that make no meaningful contributions to the world – have been called 'bullshit jobs' by the American anthropologist David Gareber. (100)

If we are honest with ourselves, most of us would have to acknowledge that the real reason we pursue a profession is that we need to make a living, or where there is a possibility to climb up the hierarchy, that it satisfies our ego that is thirsty for recognition and prestige. We are rarely willing to admit to ourselves how we live an imprisoned life, or that what we are working for is socially worthless, and eventually even harmful to others.

This state of affairs is a giant matrix, a network of social conditionings that is strongly tied to an economic order from which it is not easy to separate oneself and become self-sufficient. It is, on the one hand, a play in which we largely participate deluding ourselves and, on the other, it is sustained by the inherent structure and rules of our economic and educational system. Therefore, the problem is both individual and systemic.

One of the global challenges for which a lived experience through an FPE can prepare the future generation much better than conventional schools can is the field of economy and finance from the perspective of an ecologically sustainable model. This is because, more than ever, these will require critical, original and creative thinking to find new original and creative solutions – and there can be no true creativity and originality without true freedom.

We live in a world of commercial barbarism, where a savage, self-destructive exploitation of natural resources is the norm. There is also an ever-increasing divide between the super-rich people, who continue to become richer, and the poorest of the poor, who become even poorer. In the long run, this can't be a sustainable economic and financial model. Such a self-destructive approach to Nature also causes climate change. This predatory behavior, which razes everything it encounters in its path, is the main reason for – and the driving force behind – the mass migrations of millions of poor and desperate people.

So what does this have to do with education? Maybe egoism and greed are so deeply engraved in humanity's nature that they can't be rooted out simply by conceiving of a different school system. We should not be so naïve as to believe that. However, this should not hide the fact that our education system more or less indirectly and implicitly stands behind and nurtures this very same economic financial system. What do people otherwise mean when they say that school and college should prepare one for a future job? On what principles are these jobs based if not those that govern our actual financial system? How does the conventional job-oriented school system work? By collaboration or competition? Are the values that stand behind the idea of preparing young people for their future jobs those of liberté, égalité, fraternité?

In conventional schools, and also in most of the so-called alternative and "free" schools, not much encourages these principles. Children attend schools which rely more on principles of competition, selection and consequent segregation between good and bad students. This is something which is automatically determined by high or low grades and by whether or not one has passed one's examinations. On top of that, mobbing in schools has become a pandemic phenomenon. Where do children learn fraternity? Do we teach children in schools to work for a collective common well-being or to strive for their own interests and self-assertion? Do we foster an extrinsic motivation that works with grades, examinations and certificates, cooperation? And does this encourage and inspire responsibility or irresponsibility? Are children taught respect for Nature or indifference to Nature?

In an FPE environment where the freedom of the self-unfoldment of one's inner being is the dominant and central principle inside a non-hierarchical administration and consensus structure where learning occurs not by compulsion but by intrinsic motivation, all these negative aspects plaguing the conventional pedagogical paradigm may not disappear entirely. However, they will, at least, no longer be the driving force in the first place.

Competition is replaced by a spontaneous co-creative cooperation, e.g. by common project-oriented learning, bar camps or open-space meetings where the egoistic interests of self-assertion over others are replaced by common interest with others inside project-oriented cooperation. Selection criteria and implicit segregation into good and bad students judged by grades and examinations which set the background for a qualitative comparison can be replaced by competence portfolios. Through this approach, one focusses on one's own individual strengths instead of on weaknesses. Indifference to the environment, or the too superficial bookish knowledge of the natural cosmos, is replaced by a lived experience in contact with Nature itself.

However, this can be done only if we have the determination and courage to abolish curricula, grades, examinations and certificates and to open the system to more advanced and effective learning and teaching methods as well as more efficient systems of evaluation. Only by replacing compulsion with freedom of self-expression can children and students, as grown-up researchers, learn to express themselves, their soul factor, by developing their psychological and creative skills. Only if we replace a hierarchical system with a non-hierarchical (or sociocratic) system that allows freedom but also asks for more (not less) individual responsibility can we can hope to raise personalities that will also become more responsible with others and Nature. Only if the educational environment encourages and fosters empathy, compassion and communion can we hope that the next generation, once grown up and taking economic and political command, will have less voracious and barbaric attitudes towards practicing finance and economy and their relation to Nature.

The bottom line is that a coercive, authoritarian and hierarchical system always encourages and inevitably imprints in people's minds all these negative and selfish values typical of a predatory and irresponsible financial and economic system. This is because it is in its very intrinsic essence. If we want a human sustainable and fair trade economic financial system, there will be no way around it: We will have to switch over to a free non-authoritarian education system which emphasizes individual potential, creativity, inspiration and inner values instead of material values. If this does not occur and we maintain the current system and structure as it is, we will hardly be led to a generation of grownups who have more empathy and a sense of collective well-being.

Another example of how an FPE paradigm can be effective in raising a new generation able to tackle modern global challenges is that of conflict resolution. In times when authoritarian tendencies resurface and anti-democratic ideas seem to gain ground, a non-authoritarian and truly democratic – eventually sociocratic – education model is necessary more than anything else.

This myth which says that schools are places where children learn to socialize by learning to peacefully resolve conflicts with each other has been contradicted by facts and proven to be false over and over again. There is virtually no school which does not have to confront mobbing cases. A phenomenon frequently related to this is the numerous school shootings that have taken place worldwide, but especially in US schools. It is a well-known fact that several Islamic terrorists did not come from a background of poverty or ignorance; rather, they were well-educated, sometimes even in high-ranking western institutions. The same can be said of the leftist terrorist organization of 1970s Europe, whose ideology was, in some instances, more or less openly encouraged by academic figures. Sometimes even dictators were educated in educational institutions of advanced democratic countries, though nothing suggests that they learned anything about democratic values. For example, the couple of years that North Korean dictator Kim Jong Un spent in a Swiss school at the age of 14 do not seem to have taught him the values of democracy and human rights.

Bookish learning of democratic principles won't be very effective in transmitting these values. This is because democracy, including respect for others, human rights and human values, must become an everyday experience and practice, not just an abstract and sterile notion to learn from books. We must change the school and university system structure at its foundation, from the bottom up, and transform it from a fundamentally authoritarian structure based on a hierarchical mindset to a democratic – or eventually sociocratic – way of life, into a context where freedom and individual rights are part of the practice. Only where democracy and tolerance are lived experiences composing part of the learning path, in a context which balances freedom and responsibility by teaching means of living in unity in diversity, can a generation become capable of conflict resolution

Could then an FPE initiative be the solution? I'm quite convinced it could be, if not the only solution, certainly a great part of it. Education is a key factor which can no longer remain stalled in its medieval state of development. Whether it will work out in the format presented here, only future will tell for sure. But this is not decisive. What really matters at this stage is to look forward, to begin to have a vision of the future, to experiment, by trial-and-error methods, with failures and defeats, but at least with an attempt to go forward, instead of remaining stuck in the present. The main scope, aim, and target should be the liberation of the inner spirit, of the individual potential, of the real soul in us.

Those who have read so far, and are already engaged with modern alternative forms of pedagogy, might have recognized several aspects and recipes for a progressive form of education already outlined elsewhere. However, the word 'pedagogy' usually refers to education in primary schools, sometimes secondary schools, but never to a high school, college, or university. If humanity wants to progress towards a society of free-minded people and original and creative thinkers, this divide must fall. That is one of the reasons we are still, and have remained for too long, in the Stone Age of education. But this is also the fascinating part of all that. It is clear that much more than a reform is necessary, and that a revolutionary and radical transformation is possible. This present proposal for an FPE paradigm has to be considered only a sketch, a rough idea and a blueprint, it has no pretension to be either ultimate nor exhaustive, even not necessarily correct. But it is also a vision and dream! The main aim of these proposals has been to generate thinking on the subject. If they lead to action, then the objective of this 'manifesto' will have been amply fulfilled. Everyone interested in contributing to this 'adventure of consciousness' is encouraged to participate.

And, last but not least, I will be immensely grateful if you post a Reader Review on the book's product page at the online bookstore where you purchased it. These reviews are an essential resource to understand if and how the message came through and if it resonates with you.

Thank you! — Marco

Endnote

In developing the concept of FPE, the author was partly inspired by the teachings of the Indian poet and spiritual master Sri Aurobindo and his spiritual partner Mirra Alfassa, also called 'the Mother'. In particular, the latter developed the concept of an 'integral education' and first coined the expression "free progress education". Also, the idea of a University of Human Unity was fully adopted here as it was originally formulated by Mirra Alfassa. However, apart from that, the author, despite having immersed himself in their teachings before the appearance of this document, knew almost nothing about their integral education idea. Almost everything, apart from a few amendments and clarifications that followed later, arises from his own experience and is a formulation of it into an intellectual and secular pedagogical vision. Believe it or not, and as incredible and implausible as it might sound, he only later discovered the same principles to be formulated in their teachings from a spiritual and metaphysical perspective. The advantage of the present work is that it points out how no particular faith, in a spiritual or transcendent construct, is necessary to put into practice the principles of an FPE. Also, the idea of a soul and 'soul growth' isn't necessarily something one must take literally as a metaphysical statement. Instead, it can be intended as a psychological growth of our mind and feelings in the sense that modern scientific psychology intends. FPE is a gift to humanity as a whole, well beyond some spiritual teaching, creed or personal conviction about life and the cosmos.

Acknowledgements

I'm particularly grateful to Allan Bailur who reviewed this document by making a careful proofread and by adding also several helpful suggestions. Without his help this book would probably never have been published!

For input of various kinds I am grateful to Wagish Kumar Rai who has provided invaluable insights and support not only for this book but also to the online project of FPE.

Special thanks also to Brendan Heidenreich for his proof-reading, suggestions and for having pointed out some interesting initiatives of self-directed-education I was not aware of.

Bibliography

1. Student Loan Debt In 2017: A $1.3 Trillion Crisis. *Forbes.* [Online] 23 Feb. 2017. https://www.forbes.com/sites/zackfriedman/2017/02/21/student-loan-debt-statistics-2017/.

2. Gray, Peter. Children's & Teens' Suicides Related to the School Calendar. *Psychology Today.* [Online] 2018. https://www.psychologytoday.com/us/blog/freedom-learn/201805/children-s-teens-suicides-related-the-school-calendar.

3. *Work organization and mental health problems in PhD students.* K. Levecquea, F. Anseela, A. De Beuckelaerd, J. Van der Heydenf, L. Gisle. [ed.] Elsevier. 4, May 2017, Research Policy, Vol. 46, pp. 868-879.

4. Dodgson, Lindsay. PhD students have double the risk of developing a psychiatric disorder than the rest of the 'highly educated' population. *Business Insider UK.* [Online] 8 Auguts 2017. http://www.businessinsider.de/phd-students-could-face-significant-mental-health-problems-2017-8?r=US&IR=T.

5. *Mental health and suicidal behavior among graduate students.* Garcia-Williams, Moffitt L, Kaslow NJ. 5, s.l. : Springer, October 2014, Academic Psychiatry, Vol. 38, pp. 554-60.

6. *Understanding mental health in the research environment: A Rapid Evidence Assessment.* al., Susan Guthrie et. s.l. : Santa Monica, CA: RAND Corporation, 2017.

7. Kemsley, Jyllian. Grappling with graduate student mental health and suicide. *Chemical & Engineering News.* [Online] 7 Auguts 2017. http://cen.acs.org/articles/95/i32/Grappling-graduate-student-mental-health.html.

8. Grant, Andrew. A paper on field theory delivers a wake-up call to academics. *Physics Today.* [Online] 3 Auguts 2017. http://physicstoday.scitation.org/do/10.1063/PT.6.2.20170803a/full/.

9. Smolin, Lee. *The Trouble with Physics.* s.l. : Houghton Mifflin Harcourt, 2006.

10. Peter Higgs: I wouldn't be productive enough for today's academic system. [Online] The Guardian, 6 December 2013. www.theguardian.com/science/2013/06/peter-higgs-boson-academic-system.

11. *Deep Impact: Unintended consequences of journal rank.* Björn Brembs, Marcus Munafò. 7:291, s.l. : Frontier in Human Neuroscience, 2013, Vol. 24.

12. *'Novel, amazing, innovative': positive words on the rise in science papers.* Ball, Philip. s.l. : Nature, December 2015.

13. *Beall's list of predatory journals and publishers.* [Online] https://beallslist.weebly.com/.

14. A 2017 Nobel laureate says he left science because he ran out of money and was fed up with academia. *Quartz Media LLC.* [Online] http://www.cell.com/current-biology/fulltext/S0960-9822(07)02369-X.

15. Nobel winner declares boycott of top science journals. [Online] The Guardian, 9 December 2013. www.theguardian.com/science/2013/dec/nobel-winner-boycott-science-journals.

16. Sinkjær, Thomas. Fund ideas, not pedigree, to find fresh insight. *Nature.* [Online] https://www.nature.com/articles/d41586-018-02743-2.

17. Moore, R. L. Challange in the classroom (part 2) - At 11min 50s. [Online] Washington, DC : Mathematical Association of America : Committee on Educational Media, 1966. https://www.youtube.com/watch?v=menT1EPuHuE.

18. Jobs, Steve. Steve Jobs' 2005 Stanford Commencement Address. [Online] www.youtube.com/watch?v=UF8uR6Z6KLc.

19. Gates, Bill. *The Road Ahead.* s.l. : Penguin Books, 1996.

20. *Life is complicated.* Hayden, Erika Check. 1 April 2010, Nature, Vol. 464, p. 664.

21. Stem cells: what happened to the radical breakthroughs? [Online] The Observer, Sunday 11 August 2013. http://www.theguardian.com/science/2013/aug/11/stem-cell-research-bioengineering.

22. Chinese scientists condemn 'crazy' and 'unethical' gene-editing experiment. *South China Morning Post.* [Online] 26 November 2018. https://www.scmp.com/news/china/society/article/2175105/chinese-scientists-condemn-crazy-and-unethical-gene-editing.

23. Ledford, Heidi. CRISPR gene editing produces unwanted DNA deletions. *Nature.* [Online] 16 July 2018.

24. Kaiser, Jocelyn. The gene editor CRISPR won't fully fix sick people anytime soon. *Science.* [Online] May 2016.

25. Richard Harris. *Rigor Mortis: How Sloppy Science Creates Worthless Cures, Crushes Hope, and Wastes Billions.* s.l. : Basic Books, 2017.

26. Hosselfelder, Sabine. Merchants of Hype. *Backreaction.* [Online] March 2019. https://backreaction.blogspot.com/2019/03/merchants-of-hype.html.

27. The Human Brain Project. [Online] http://www.humanbrainproject.eu/introduction.html.

28. Open message to the European Commission. [Online] http://neurofuture.eu/.

29. The Case Against Quantum Computing. *IEEE.* [Online] November 2018. https://spectrum.ieee.org/computing/hardware/the-case-against-quantum-computing.

30. *Supersymmetry and the Crisis in Physics.* May, 2014, Scientific American Magazine.

31. What No New Particles Means for Physics. *Quanta Magazine.* [Online] 9 August 2016. https://www.quantamagazine.org/what-no-new-particles-means-for-physics-20160809.

32. Fortin J-M, Currie DJ. Big Science vs. Little Science: How Scientific Impact Scales with Funding. [Online] 2013. http://www.plosone.org/article/info%3Adoi%2F10.1371%2Fjournal.pone.0065263#authcontrib.

33. Simonton, Dean Keith. After Einstein: Scientific genius is extinct. *Nature.* 2013, Vol. 493, 7434.

34. Oral History Transcript — Sir James Chadwick. Niels Bohr Library & Archives, American Institute of Physics. [Online] http://www.aip.org/history/ohilist/3974_3.html.

35. American Institute of Physics's Center for History of Physics, "Rutherford's nuclear world". [Online] http://www.aip.org/.

36. Nicholas Bloom, Charles I. Jones, John Van Reenen, Michael Webb. Are Ideas Getting Harder to Find? *National Bureau of Economic Research.* Working Paper No. 23782, 2017.

37. Keynes, John Maynard. *Economic Possibilities for our Grandchildren.* 1930.

38. Methodos. [Online] http://methodos-ev.org/.

39. Ciobanu, Alia. *Revolution im Klassenzimmer - Wenn Schüler ihre eigene Schule gründen.* s.l. : Herder GmbH, 2012.

40. Rousseau, Jean-Jacques. *"Emile, or On Education" (original French edition: "Émile, ou De l'éducation").* 1762.

41. Shams L., Seitz AR. Benefits of multisensory learning. *Trends Cogn Sci.* 2008, 12(11):411-7.

42. Thomas Beery, Kari Anne Jørgensen. Children in nature: sensory engagement and the experience of biodiversity. 2018, 24:1, 13-25.

43. Dewey, John. *My Pedagogic Creed.* 1897.

44. TED / Ideas worth spreading. [Online] http://www.ted.com/.

45. Helfand, David. Designing a university for the new millennium. [Online] https://www.youtube.com/watch?v=DZQe73IXZtU.

46. Gilbert, Elizabeth. Elizabeth Gilbert: Your elusive creative genius. [Online] 2009. http://www.ted.com/talks/elizabeth_gilbert_on_genius.html.

47. Leadbeater, Charles. Education innovation in the slums. [Online] 2010. http://www.ted.com/talks/charles_leadbeater_on_education.html.

48. Cain, Susan. The power of introverts. [Online] 2012. http://www.ted.com/talks/susan_cain_the_power_of_introverts.html.

49. —. The Rise of the New Groupthink. *Opinion section of The New York Times.* 13 January 2012.

50. *Neuroscience and education: prime time to build the bridge.* Mariano Sigman, Marcela Peña, Andrea P Goldin and Sidarta Ribeiro. 17, 2014, Nature Neuroscience, pp. 497–502.

51. Hüther, Gerald. The Neurobiological Preconditions for the Development of Curiosity and Creativity. [Online] http://www.gerald-huether.de/pdf/neurobiological_preconditions.pdf.

52. Center for Contempaltive Mind in Society. [Online] http://www.contemplativemind.org/.

53. Horn, Heather Staker and Michael B. Classifying K–12 Blended Learning. [Online] 2012. http://www.innosightinstitute.org/innosight/wp-content/uploads/2012/05/Classifying-K-12-blended-learning2.pdf.

54. Khan Academy. [Online] https://www.khanacademy.org/.

55. Mitra, Sugata. TED Weekends; The SOLE challenge. [Online] http://www.ted.com/pages/sole_challenge#download.

56. Kamenetz, Anya. *DIY U: Edupunks, Edupreneurs, and the Coming Transformation of Higher Education.* s.l. : Chelsea Green Publishing, 2010.

57. *Lernen durch Lehren.* Jean-Pol Martin, Guido Oebel. 2007, Deutschunterricht in Japan (Zeitschrift des Japanischen Lehrerverbandes), Bd. 12, S. 4-21.

58. Lernen durch Lehren. [Online] www.ldl.de.

59. Udemy. [Online] https://www.udemy.com/.

60. The Kin School Tekos Russia. [Online] https://www.youtube.com/watch?v=d94TIzrtQhM.

61. Mysteries of the Lightfall - a unique school in Tekos. [Online] https://www.youtube.com/watch?v=YW2lFeNkLLM.

62. Lais Canada Natural Learning. [Online] http://www.laiscanada.com/.

63. Lais South Africa. [Online] https://laissouthafrica.wordpress.com/.

64. Lais Schule - Natürliches Lernen. [Online] http://www.laisschule.at/.

65. Lais Institut aus Klagenfurt. [Online] http://www.lais-institut.net/.

66. *Uniexperiment.* [Online] https://uniexperiment.wordpress.com/.

67. Swaraj University. [Online] http://www.swarajuniversity.org.

68. Kaospilot. [Online] http://www.kaospilot.dk.

69. Knowmads. [Online] http://www.knowmads.nl.

70. *Open Master's Community.* [Online] https://www.openmasters.org/.

71. Education Revolution - Alternative Education Resource Organization. [Online] http://www.educationrevolution.org/store/resources/alternatives/.

72. Gray, Peter. *Free to Learn: Why Unleashing the Instinct to Play Will Make Our Children Happier, More Self-Reliant, and Better Students for Life.* s.l. : Basic Books, 2015.

73. The Alliance for Self-Directed Education. [Online] https://www.self-directed.org/.

74. *Agile Learning Centers.* [Online] http://agilelearningcenters.org/.

75. *Northstarteens.* [Online] http://www.northstarteens.org/.

76. Robinson, Sir Ken. [Online] http://sirkenrobinson.com/.

77. TED. Do schools kill creativity? [Online] https://www.youtube.com/watch?v=iG9CE55wbtY.

78. *The Challenges and Benefits of Unschooling, According to 232 Families Who Have Chosen that Route.* Riley, Peter Gray and Gina. 14, 2013, Journal of Unschooling and Alternative Learning, Vol. 7.

79. Gray, Peter. A Survey of Grown Unschoolers I: Overview of Findings. Seventy-five unschooled adults report on their childhood and adult experiences. *Psychology Today.* 2014.

80. *Exploring Academic Outcomes of Homeschooled Students.* Cogan, Michael F. Sum 2010, Journal of College Admission, pp. n208 p18-25.

81. Wile, Dr. Jay L. Homeschooling: Discovering How and Why It Works. [Online] http://www.drwile.com/hs_how_why.pdf.

82. List of homeschooled people. *Wikipedia.* [Online] https://en.wikipedia.org/wiki/List_of_homeschooled_people.

83. Gray, Peter. The Culture of Childhood: We've Almost Destroyed It. [Online] https://www.psychologytoday.com/blog/freedom-learn/201610/the-culture-childhood-we-ve-almost-destroyed-it.

84. *The decline of play and the rise of psychopathology in childhood and adolescence.* Gray, Peter. 3, s.l. : American Journal of Play, 2011, pp. 443-463.

85. Gray, Peter. The Decline of Play and Rise in Children's Mental Disorders. [Online] https://www.psychologytoday.com/blog/freedom-learn/201001/the-decline-play-and-rise-in-childrens-mental-disorders.

86. —. The play deficit. *Aeon.* [Online] 2013. https://aeon.co/essays/children-today-are-suffering-a-severe-deficit-of-play.

87. *Children's views on their lives and well-being in 15 countries: A report on the Children's Worlds survey.* s.l. : Jacobs Foundation, 2013-2014.

88. SchulFrei Bewegung. [Online] https://schulfrei-bewegung.de/.

89. Greenberg, Daniel. *Free at Last: The Sudbury Valley School.* 1991 : ISBN 1-888947-00-4.

90. Ken Robinson, Lou Aronica. *The Element: How Finding Your Passion Changes Everything.* s.l. : Penguin Books, 2009.

91. Wagner, Tony. Tony Wagner's Seven Survival Skills. [Online] http://www.tonywagner.com/7-survival-skills.

92. Roksa, Richard Arum and Josipa. *Academically Adrift: Limited Learning on College Campuses.* s.l. : University of Chicago Press, 2011.

93. *Barriers to Change: The Real Reason Behind the Kodak Downfall.* Kotter, John. MAY 2, 2012, Forbes.

94. David W. Johnson Ed.D., Roger T. Johnson Ed.D., Dean Tjosvold Ph.D. *Effective Cooperation, The Foundation of Sustainable Peace.* s.l. : Psychological Components of Sustainable Peace, Peace Psychology Book Series 2012, pp 15-53, Springer., 2012.

95. Parker J. Palmer, Arthur Zajonc, Megan Scribner. *The Heart of Higher Education: a Call to Renewal.* s.l. : Jossey-Bass, 2010.

96. Open source learning. *Wikipedia.* [Online] https://en.wikipedia.org/wiki/Open-source_learning.

97. IBL at Sheffield. [Online] University of Sheffield. http://www.sheffield.ac.uk/ibl.

98. Sociocracy. [Online] http://www.sociocracy.info/.

99. Rainbow Mountain Childern's School. [Online] http://rainbowcommunityschool.org/.

100. Ackoff, Russell. System thinking speech. [Online] https://www.youtube.com/watch?v=EbLh7rZ3rhU.

101. *Wayfinding Academy.* [Online] https://wayfindingacademy.org/.

102. Masi, M. Transcript from a Cosmos Cafe talk on FPE. [Online] https://www.youtube.com/watch?v=fGIXndMRzcU&t=10s.

103. Graeber, David. *Bullshit Jobs.* s.l. : Simon & Schuster.

*About the author

Marco Masi was born in 1965 and attended the German School of Milan, Italy. He graduated in physics at the university of Padua, and later obtained a Ph.D. in physics at the university of Trento. He worked as a postdoc researcher in universities in Italy, France, and more recently in Germany, where he worked also as a school teacher for three years. After  he had authored some scientific papers (http://ow.ly/snz6u), his interests veered towards new forms of individual learning and a new concept of FPE originated from his activity both as a tutor in several universities and as a high school teacher, but especially from his direct, lived experience of what education should not be. From this originated his desire to write this book on education. He is also interested in metaphysical and philosophical ruminations and loves walking in the woods.

Contact information
    Personal contact
Email: marco.masi@gmail.com

FPE Channels

Website: https://freeprogresseducation.org/

YouTube:
https://www.youtube.com/channel/UCSbM1KXqXkEvPGaCP2CYyEQ

Facebook: https://www.facebook.com/groups/850174021796251/

Twitter: https://twitter.com/freeprogressedu

www.ingramcontent.com/pod-product-compliance
Lightning Source LLC
Chambersburg PA
CBHW071752120626
46550CB00002B/762